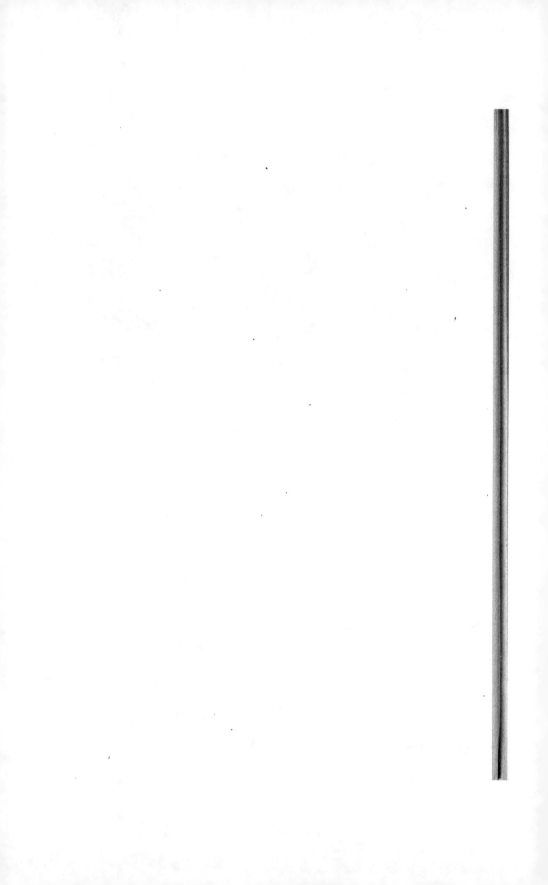

CITIZENSHIP AND SOCIAL CLASS

AND OTHER ESSAYS

CITIZENSHIP AND SOCIAL CLASS

and other essays

BY

T. H. MARSHALL

Professor of Social Institutions in the
University of London

CAMBRIDGE
AT THE UNIVERSITY PRESS
1950

PUBLISHED BY
THE SYNDICS OF THE CAMBRIDGE UNIVERSITY PRESS
London Office: Bentley House, N.W. I
American Branch: New York

Agents for Canada, India, and Pakistan: Macmillan

Printed in Great Britain at the University Press, Cambridge
(Brooke Crutchley, University Printer)

To

NADINE

CONTENTS

PREFACE

THE first half of this book is based on two lectures given at Cambridge on the Alfred Marshall foundation in February 1949. When I had got some way with the preparation of the lectures, I found that the subject I had chosen was too large for the time allowed me, and I therefore wrote a second and briefer version, omitting several points and passages from the first draft. In preparing the lectures for publication I have amalgamated the two versions and also somewhat expanded sections where the argument appeared to be too condensed. I have not, however, altered their general character as lectures designed for a mixed audience, mainly of undergraduates, nor have I attempted to bring them up to date by adding references to events which have occurred or publications which have appeared since the lectures were delivered.

The three additional chapters have all been published before. I include them because they represent my earlier thoughts on very closely related topics and to some extent fill gaps in the lectures. I am indebted to the Editors of *The Sociological Review* and *The Canadian Journal of Economics and Political Science* and to the Institute of Sociology for permission to reprint them.

T. H. MARSHALL

THE LONDON SCHOOL
OF ECONOMICS

August 1949

CITIZENSHIP AND SOCIAL CLASS

1. *The Problem stated, with the assistance of Alfred Marshall*

THE invitation to deliver these lectures gave me both personal and professional pleasure. But, whereas my personal response was a sincere and modest appreciation of an honour I had no right to expect, my professional reaction was not modest at all. Sociology, it seemed to me, had every right to claim a share in this annual commemoration of Alfred Marshall, and I considered it a sign of grace that a University which has not yet accepted sociology as an inmate should nevertheless be prepared to welcome her as a visitor. It may be—and the thought is a disturbing one—that sociology is on trial here in my person. If so, I am sure I can rely on you to be scrupulously fair in your judgement, and to regard any merit you may find in my lectures as evidence of the academic value of the subject I profess, while treating everything in them that appears to you paltry, common or ill-conceived as the product of qualities peculiar to myself and not to be found in any of my colleagues.

I will not defend the relevance of my subject to the occasion by claiming Marshall as a sociologist. For, once he had deserted his first loves of metaphysics, ethics and psychology, he devoted his life to the development of economics as an independent science and to the perfection of its own special methods of investigation and analysis. He deliberately chose a path markedly different from that followed by Adam Smith and John Stuart Mill, and the mood in which he made this choice is indicated in the inaugural lecture which he delivered here in Cambridge in 1885. Speaking of Comte's belief in a unified social science, he said: 'No doubt if that existed Economics would gladly find shelter under its wing. But it does not exist; it shows no signs of coming into existence. There is no use in waiting idly for it; we must do what we can with our present resources.'[1] He therefore defended the autonomy and the superiority of the economic method, a superiority due mainly to its use of the measuring rod of money, which 'is so much the best measure of motives that no other can compete with it'.[2]

Marshall was, as you know, an idealist; so much so that Keynes has said of him that he 'was too anxious to do good'.[3] The last thing I wish to do is to claim him for sociology on that account. It is true that some sociologists have suffered from a similar affliction of benevolence, often to the detriment of their intellectual performance, but I should hate to distinguish the economist from the sociologist by saying that the one should be ruled by his head while the other may be swayed by his heart. For every honest sociologist, like every honest economist, knows that the choice of ends or ideals lies outside the field of social science and within the field of social philo-

[1] *Memorials of Alfred Marshall*, edited by A. C. Pigou, p. 164.
[2] *Ib.* p. 158.   [3] *Ib.* p. 37.

sophy. But idealism made Marshall passionately eager to put the science of economics at the service of policy by using it—as a science may legitimately be used—to lay bare the full nature and content of the problems with which policy has to deal and to assess the relative efficacy of alternative means for the achievement of given ends. And he realised that, even in the case of what would naturally be regarded as economic problems, the science of economics was not of itself able fully to render these two services. For they involved the consideration of social forces which are as immune to attack by the economist's tape-measure as was the croquet ball to the blows which Alice tried in vain to strike with the head of her flamingo. It was, perhaps, on this account that, in certain moods, Marshall felt a quite unwarranted disappointment at his achievements, and even expressed regret that he had preferred economics to psychology, a science which might have brought him nearer to the pulse and life-blood of society and given him a deeper understanding of human aspirations.

It would be easy to cite many passages in which Marshall was drawn to speak of these elusive factors of whose importance he was so firmly convinced, but I prefer to confine my attention to one essay whose theme comes very near to that which I have chosen for these lectures. It is a paper he read to the Cambridge Reform Club in 1873 on *The Future of the Working Classes*, and it has been republished in the Memorial volume edited by Professor Pigou. There are some textual differences between the two editions which, I understand, are to be attributed to corrections made by Marshall himself after the original version had appeared in print as a pamphlet.[1] I was reminded of this essay by my colleague, Professor Phelps Brown, who made use of it in his inaugural lecture last November.[2] It is equally well suited to my purpose to-day, because in it Marshall, while examining one facet of the problem of social equality from the point of view of economic cost, came right up to the frontier beyond which lies the territory of sociology, crossed it, and made a brief excursion on the other side. His action could be interpreted as a challenge to sociology to send an emissary to meet him at the frontier, and to join with him in the task of converting no-man's-land into common ground. I have been presumptuous enough to answer the challenge by setting out to travel, as historian and sociologist, towards a point on the economic frontier of that same general theme, the problem of social equality.

In his Cambridge paper Marshall posed the question 'whether there be valid ground for the opinion that the amelioration of the working classes has limits beyond which it cannot pass'. 'The question', he said, 'is not whether all men will ultimately be equal—that they certainly will not—but whether progress may not go on steadily, if slowly, till, by occupation at least, every man is a gentleman. I hold that it may, and that it will.'[3] His faith was based on the belief that the distinguishing

[1] Privately printed by Thomas Tofts. The page references are to this edition.

[2] Published under the title "Prospects of Labour" in *Economica*, February 1949.

[3] *Op. cit.* pp. 3 and 4.

feature of the working classes was heavy and excessive labour, and that the volume of such labour could be greatly reduced. Looking round he found evidence that the skilled artisans, whose labour was not deadening and soul-destroying, were already rising towards the condition which he foresaw as the ultimate achievement of all. They are learning, he said, to value education and leisure more than 'mere increase of wages and material comforts'. They are 'steadily developing independence and a manly respect for themselves and, therefore, a courteous respect for others; they are steadily accepting the private and public duties of a citizen; steadily increasing their grasp of the truth that they are men, and not producing machines. They are steadily becoming gentlemen.'[1] When technical advance has reduced heavy labour to a minimum, and that minimum is divided in small amounts among all, then, 'in so far as the working classes are men who have such excessive work to do, in so far will the working classes have been abolished.'[2]

Marshall realised that he might be accused of adopting the ideas of the socialists, whose works, as he has himself told us, he had, during this period of his life, been studying with great hopes and with greater disappointment. For, he said: 'The picture to be drawn will resemble in some respects those which have been shown to us by the Socialists, that noble set of untutored enthusiasts who attributed to all men an unlimited capacity for those self-forgetting virtues that they found in their own

[1] *The Future of the Working Classes*, p. 6.　　[2] *Ib.* p. 16.

breasts.'[1] His reply was that his system differed fundamentally from socialism in that it would preserve the
essentials of a free market. He held, however, that the
State would have to make some use of its power of com-
pulsion, if his ideals were to be realised. It must compel
children to go to school, because the uneducated cannot
appreciate, and therefore freely choose, the good things
which distinguish the life of gentlemen from that of the
working classes. 'It is bound to compel them and to help
them to take the first step upwards; and it is bound to
help them, if they will, to make many steps upwards.'[2]
Notice that only the first step is compulsory. Free choice
takes over as soon as the capacity to choose has been
created.

Marshall's paper was built round a sociological hypothesis and an economic calculation. The calculation provided the answer to his initial question, by showing that
world resources and productivity might be expected to
prove sufficient to provide the material bases needed to
enable every man to be a gentleman. In other words, the
cost of providing education for all and of eliminating
heavy and excessive labour could be met. There was no
impassable limit to the amelioration of the working
classes—at least on this side of the point that Marshall

[1] *The Future of the Working Classes*, p. 9. The revised version of
this passage is significantly different. It runs: 'The picture to be drawn
will resemble in many respects those which have been shown to us by
some socialists, who attributed to all men...' etc. The condemnation
is less sweeping and Marshall no longer speaks of the Socialists,
en masse and with a capital 'S', in the past tense. *Memorials*, p. 109.
[2] *Ib.* p. 15.

described as the goal. In working out these sums Marshall was using the ordinary techniques of the economist, though admittedly he was applying them to a problem which involved a high degree of speculation.

The sociological hypothesis does not lie so completely on the surface. A little excavation is needed to uncover its total shape. The essence of it is contained in the passages I have quoted, but Marshall gives us an additional clue by suggesting that, when we say a man belongs to the working classes, 'we are thinking of the effect that his work produces on him rather than the effect that he produces on his work'.[1] This is certainly not the sort of definition we should expect from an economist, and, in fact, it would hardly be fair to treat it as a definition at all or to subject it to close and critical examination. The phrase was intended to catch the imagination, and to point to the general direction in which Marshall's thoughts were moving. And that direction was away from a quantitative assessment of standards of living in terms of goods consumed and services enjoyed towards a qualitative assessment of life as a whole in terms of the essential elements in civilisation or culture. He accepted as right and proper a wide range of quantitative or economic inequality, but condemned the qualitative inequality or difference between the man who was, 'by occupation at least, a gentleman' and the man who was not. We can, I think, without doing violence to Marshall's meaning, replace the word 'gentleman' by the word 'civilised'. For it is clear that he was taking as the standard of civilised life

[1] *Ib.* p. 5.

the conditions regarded by his generation as appropriate to a gentleman. We can go on to say that the claim of all to enjoy these conditions is a claim to be admitted to a share in the social heritage, which in turn means a claim to be accepted as full members of the society, that is, as citizens.

Such, I think, is the sociological hypothesis latent in Marshall's essay. It postulates that there is a kind of basic human equality associated with the concept of full membership of a community—or, as I should say, of citizenship—which is not inconsistent with the inequalities which distinguish the various economic levels in the society. In other words, the inequality of the social class system may be acceptable provided the equality of citizenship is recognised. Marshall did not identify the life of a gentleman with the status of citizenship. To do so would have been to express his ideal in terms of legal rights to which all men were entitled. That, in turn, would have put the responsibility for granting those rights fair and square on the shoulders of the State, and so led, step by step, to acts of State interference which he would have deplored. When he mentioned citizenship as something which skilled artisans learned to appreciate in the course of developing into gentlemen, he mentioned only its duties and not its rights. He thought of it as a way of life growing within a man, not presented to him from without. He recognised only one definite right, the right of children to be educated, and in this case alone did he approve the use of compulsory powers by the State to achieve his object. He could hardly go further without imperilling

8

his own criterion for distinguishing his system from socialism in any form—the preservation of the freedom of the competitive market.

Nevertheless, his sociological hypothesis lies as near to the heart of our problem to-day as it did three-quarters of a century ago—in fact nearer. The basic human equality of membership, at which I maintain that he hinted, has been enriched with new substance and invested with a formidable array of rights. It has developed far beyond what he foresaw, or would have wished. It has been clearly identified with the status of citizenship. And it is time we examined his hypothesis and posed his questions afresh, to see if the answers are still the same. Is it still true that basic equality, when enriched in substance and embodied in the formal rights of citizenship, is consistent with the inequalities of social class? I shall suggest that our society to-day assumes that the two are still compatible, so much so that citizenship has itself become, in certain respects, the architect of legitimate social inequality. Is it still true that the basic equality can be created and preserved without invading the freedom of the competitive market? Obviously it is not true. Our modern system is frankly a socialist system, not one whose authors are, as Marshall was, eager to distinguish it from socialism. But it is equally obvious that the market still functions—within limits. Here is another possible conflict of principles which demands examination. And thirdly, what is the effect of the marked shift of emphasis from duties to rights? Is this an inevitable feature of modern citizenship—inevitable and irreversible?

9

Finally, I want to put Marshall's initial question again in a new form. He asked if there were limits beyond which the amelioration of the working classes could not pass, and he was thinking of limits set by natural resources and productivity. I shall ask whether there appear to be limits beyond which the modern drive towards social equality cannot, or is unlikely to, pass, and I shall be thinking, not of the economic cost (I leave that vital question to the economists), but of the limits inherent in the principles that inspire the drive. But the modern drive towards social equality is, I believe, the latest phase of an evolution of citizenship which has been in continuous progress for some 250 years. My first task, therefore, must be to prepare the ground for an attack on the problems of to-day by digging for a while in the subsoil of past history.

2. *The Development of Citizenship to the end of the Nineteenth Century*

I shall be running true to type as a sociologist if I begin by saying that I propose to divide citizenship into three parts. But the analysis is, in this case, dictated by history even more clearly than by logic. I shall call these three parts, or elements, civil, political and social. The civil element is composed of the rights necessary for individual freedom—liberty of the person, freedom of speech, thought and faith, the right to own property and to conclude valid contracts, and the right to justice. The last is of a different order from the others, because it is the right to defend and assert all one's rights on terms of equality with others and by due process of law. This shows us that the institutions most directly associated with civil rights are the courts of justice. By the political element I mean the right to participate in the exercise of political power, as a member of a body invested with political authority or as an elector of the members of such a body. The corresponding institutions are parliament and councils of local government. By the social element I mean the whole range from the right to a modicum of economic welfare and security to the right to share to the full in the social heritage and to live the life of a civilised being according to the standards prevailing in the society. The institutions most closely connected with it are the educational system and the social services.[1]

In early times these three strands were wound into a single thread. The rights were blended because the institutions were amalgamated. As Maitland said: 'The further back we trace our history the more impossible it is for us to draw strict lines of demarcation between the various functions of the State: the same institution is a legislative assembly, a governmental council and a court of law....Everywhere, as we pass from the ancient to the modern, we see what the fashionable philosophy calls differentiation.'[2] Maitland is speaking here of the fusion of political and civil institutions and rights. But a man's social rights, too, were part of the same amalgam, and

[1] By this terminology, what economists sometimes call 'income from civil rights' would be called 'income from social rights'. Cf. H. Dalton, *Some Aspects of the Inequality of Incomes in Modern Communities*, pt. III, chs. 3 and 4.

[2] *Constitutional History of England*, p. 105.

derived from the status which also determined the kind of justice he could get and where he could get it, and the way in which he could take part in the administration of the affairs of the community of which he was a member. But this status was not one of citizenship in our modern sense. In feudal society status was the hall-mark of class and the measure of inequality. There was no uniform collection of rights and duties with which all men—noble and common, free and serf—were endowed by virtue of their membership of the society. There was, in this sense, no principle of the equality of citizens to set against the principle of the inequality of classes. In the medieval towns, on the other hand, examples of genuine and equal citizenship can be found. But its specific rights and duties were strictly local, whereas the citizenship whose history I wish to trace is, by definition, national.

Its evolution involved a double process, of fusion and of separation. The fusion was geographical, the separation functional. The first important step dates from the twelfth century, when royal justice was established with effective power to define and defend the civil rights of the individual—such as they then were—on the basis, not of local custom, but of the common law of the land. As institutions the courts were national, but specialised. Parliament followed, concentrating in itself the political powers of national government and shedding all but a small residue of the judicial functions which formerly belonged to the Curia Regis, that 'sort of constitutional protoplasm out of which will in time be evolved the various councils of the crown, the houses of parliament, and the courts of law'.[1] Finally, the social rights which had been rooted in membership of the village community, the town and the gild were gradually dissolved by economic change until nothing remained but the Poor Law, again a specialised institution which acquired a national foundation, although it continued to be locally administered.

Two important consequences followed. First, when the institutions on which the three elements of citizenship depended parted company, it became possible for each to go its separate way, travelling at its own speed under the direction of its own peculiar principles. Before long they were spread far out along the course, and it is only in the present century, in fact I might say only within the last few months, that the three runners have come abreast of one another.

Secondly, institutions that were national and specialised could not belong so intimately to the life of the social groups they served as those that were local and of a general character. The remoteness of parliament was due to the mere size of its constituency; the remoteness of the courts, to the technicalities of their law and their procedure, which made it necessary for the citizen to employ legal experts to advise him as to the nature of his rights and to help him to obtain them. It has been pointed out again and again that, in the Middle Ages, participation in public affairs was more a duty than a right. Men owed suit and service to the court appropriate to their class and neighbourhood. The court belonged to them and they to it, and they had

[1] A. F. Pollard, *Evolution of Parliament*, p. 25.

13

access to it because it needed them and because they had knowledge of its affairs. But the result of the twin process of fusion and separation was that the machinery giving access to the institutions on which the rights of citizenship depended had to be shaped afresh. In the case of political rights the story is the familiar one of the franchise and the qualifications for membership of parliament. In the case of civil rights the issue hangs on the jurisdiction of the various courts, the privileges of the legal profession, and above all on the liability to meet the costs of litigation. In the case of social rights the centre of the stage is occupied by the Law of Settlement and Removal and the various forms of means test. All this apparatus combined to decide, not merely what rights were recognised in principle, but also to what extent rights recognised in principle could be enjoyed in practice.

When the three elements of citizenship parted company, they were soon barely on speaking terms. So complete was the divorce between them that it is possible, without doing too much violence to historical accuracy, to assign the formative period in the life of each to a different century—civil rights to the eighteenth, political to the nineteenth, and social to the twentieth. These periods must, of course, be treated with reasonable elasticity, and there is some evident overlap, especially between the last two.

To make the eighteenth century cover the formative period of civil rights it must be stretched backwards to include Habeas Corpus, the Toleration Act, and the abolition of the censorship of the press; and it must be extended forwards to include Catholic Emancipation, the repeal of the Combination Acts, and the successful end of the battle for the freedom of the press associated with the names of Cobbett and Richard Carlile. It could then be more accurately, but less briefly, described as the period between the Revolution and the first Reform Act. By the end of that period, when political rights made their first infantile attempt to walk in 1832, civil rights had come to man's estate and bore, in most essentials, the appearance that they have to-day.[1] 'The specific work of the earlier Hanoverian epoch', writes Trevelyan, 'was the establishment of the rule of law; and that law, with all its grave faults, was at least a law of freedom. On that solid foundation all our subsequent reforms were built.'[2] This eighteenth-century achievement, interrupted by the French Revolution and completed after it, was in large measure the work of the courts, both in their daily practice and also in a series of famous cases in some of which they were fighting against parliament in defence of individual liberty. The most celebrated actor in this drama was, I suppose, John Wilkes, and, although we may deplore the absence in him of those noble and saintly qualities which we should like to find in our national heroes, we cannot complain if the cause of liberty is sometimes championed by a libertine.

In the economic field the basic civil right is the right to work, that is to say the right to follow the occupation of

[1] The most important exception is the right to strike, but the conditions which made this right vital for the workman and acceptable to political opinion had not yet fully come into being.
[2] *English Social History*, p. 351.

15

one's choice in the place of one's choice, subject only to legitimate demands for preliminary technical training. This right had been denied by both statute and custom; on the one hand by the Elizabethan Statute of Artificers, which confined certain occupations to certain social classes, and on the other by local regulations reserving employment in a town to its own members and by the use of apprenticeship as an instrument of exclusion rather than of recruitment. The recognition of the right involved the formal acceptance of a fundamental change of attitude. The old assumption that local and group monopolies were in the public interest, because 'trade and traffic cannot be maintained or increased without order and government',[1] was replaced by the new assumption that such restrictions were an offence against the liberty of the subject and a menace to the prosperity of the nation. As in the case of the other civil rights, the courts of law played a decisive part in promoting and registering the advance of the new principle. The Common Law was elastic enough for the judges to apply it in a manner which, almost imperceptibly, took account of gradual changes in circumstances and opinion and eventually installed the heresy of the past as the orthodoxy of the present. The Common Law is largely a matter of common sense, as witness the judgement given by Chief Justice Holt in the case of Mayor of Winton *v.* Wilks (1705): 'All people are at liberty to live in Winchester, and how can they be

[1] City of London Case, 1610. See E. F. Heckscher, *Mercantilism*, vol. I, pp. 269–325, where the whole story is told in considerable detail.

restrained from using the lawful means of living there? Such a custom is an injury to the party and a prejudice to the public.'[1] Custom was one of the two great obstacles to the change. But, when ancient custom in the technical sense was clearly at variance with contemporary custom in the sense of the generally accepted way of life, its defences began to crumble fairly rapidly before the attacks of a Common Law which had, as early as 1614, expressed its abhorrence of 'all monopolies which prohibit any from working in any lawful trade'.[2] The other obstacle was statute law, and the judges struck some shrewd blows even against this doughty opponent. In 1756 Lord Mansfield described the Elizabethan Statute of Artificers as a penal law, in restraint of natural right and contrary to the Common Law of the kingdom. He added that 'the policy upon which the Act was made is, from experience, become doubtful'.[3]

By the beginning of the nineteenth century this principle of individual economic freedom was accepted as axiomatic. You are probably familiar with the passage quoted by the Webbs from the report of the Select Committee of 1811, which states that 'no interference of the legislature with the freedom of trade, or with the perfect liberty of every individual to dispose of his time and of his labour in the way and on the terms which he may judge most conducive to his own interest, can take place without violating general principles of the first

---

[1] *King's Bench Reports* (Holt), p. 1002.
[2] Heckscher, *op. cit.* vol. I, p. 283.
[3] *Ib.* p. 316.

importance to the prosperity and happiness of the community'.[1] The repeal of the Elizabethan statutes followed quickly, as the belated recognition of a revolution which had already taken place.

The story of civil rights in their formative period is one of the gradual addition of new rights to a status that already existed and was held to appertain to all adult members of the community—or perhaps one should say to all male members, since the status of women, or at least of married women, was in some important respects peculiar. This democratic, or universal, character of the status arose naturally from the fact that it was essentially the status of freedom, and in seventeenth-century England all men were free. Servile status, or villeinage by blood, had lingered on as a patent anachronism in the days of Elizabeth, but vanished soon afterwards. This change from servile to free labour has been described by Professor Tawney as 'a high landmark in the development both of economic and political society', and as 'the final triumph of the common law' in regions from which it had been excluded for four centuries. Henceforth the English peasant 'is a member of a society in which there is, nominally at least, one law for all men'.[2] The liberty which his predecessors had won by fleeing into the free towns had become his by right. In the towns the terms 'freedom' and 'citizenship' were interchangeable. When freedom became universal, citizenship grew from a local into a national institution.

[1] *History of Trade Unionism* (1920), p. 60.
[2] *Agrarian Problem in the Sixteenth Century*, pp. 43–4.

The story of political rights is different both in time and in character. The formative period began, as I have said, in the early nineteenth century, when the civil rights attached to the status of freedom had already acquired sufficient substance to justify us in speaking of a general status of citizenship. And, when it began, it consisted, not in the creation of new rights to enrich a status already enjoyed by all, but in the granting of old rights to new sections of the population. In the eighteenth century political rights were defective, not in content, but in distribution—defective, that is to say, by the standards of democratic citizenship. The Act of 1832 did little, in a purely quantitative sense, to remedy that defect. After it was passed the voters still amounted to less than one-fifth of the adult male population. The franchise was still a group monopoly, but it had taken the first step towards becoming a monopoly of a kind acceptable to the ideas of nineteenth-century capitalism—a monopoly which could, with some degree of plausibility, be described as open and not closed. A closed group monopoly is one into which no man can force his way by his own efforts; admission is at the pleasure of the existing members of the group. The description fits a considerable part of the borough franchise before 1832; and it is not too wide of the mark when applied to the franchise based on freehold ownership of land. Freeholds are not always to be had for the asking, even if one has the money to buy them, especially in an age in which families look on their lands as the social, as well as the economic, foundation of their existence. Therefore the Act of 1832, by abolishing rotten boroughs and by extending the franchise to leaseholders and occupying tenants of sufficient economic substance, opened the monopoly by recognising the political claims of those who could produce the normal evidence of success in the economic struggle.

It is clear that, if we maintain that in the nineteenth century citizenship in the form of civil rights was universal, the political franchise was not one of the rights of citizenship. It was the privilege of a limited economic class, whose limits were extended by each successive Reform Act. It can nevertheless be argued that citizenship in this period was not politically meaningless. It did not confer a right, but it recognised a capacity. No sane and law-abiding citizen was debarred by personal status from acquiring and recording a vote. He was free to earn, to save, to buy property or to rent a house, and to enjoy whatever political rights were attached to these economic achievements. His civil rights entitled him, and electoral reform increasingly enabled him, to do this.

It was, as we shall see, appropriate that nineteenth-century capitalist society should treat political rights as a secondary product of civil rights. It was equally appropriate that the twentieth century should abandon this position and attach political rights directly and independently to citizenship as such. This vital change of principle was put into effect when the Act of 1918, by adopting manhood suffrage, shifted the basis of political rights from economic substance to personal status. I say 'manhood' deliberately in order to emphasise the great significance of this reform quite apart from the second, and no less important, reform introduced at the same time—namely the enfranchisement of women. But the Act of 1918 did not fully establish the political equality of all in terms of the rights of citizenship. Remnants of an inequality based on differences of economic substance lingered on until, only last year, plural voting (which had already been reduced to dual voting) was finally abolished.

When I assigned the formative periods of the three elements of citizenship each to a separate century—civil rights to the eighteenth, political to the nineteenth and social to the twentieth—I said that there was a considerable overlap between the last two. I propose to confine what I have to say now about social rights to this overlap, in order that I may complete my historical survey to the end of the nineteenth century, and draw my conclusions from it, before turning my attention to the second half of my subject, a study of our present experiences and their immediate antecedents. In this second act of the drama social rights will occupy the centre of the stage.

The original source of social rights was membership of local communities and functional associations. This source was supplemented and progressively replaced by a Poor Law and a system of wage regulation which were nationally conceived and locally administered. The latter—the system of wage regulation—was rapidly decaying in the eighteenth century, not only because industrial change made it administratively impossible, but also because it was incompatible with the new conception of civil rights in the economic sphere, with its emphasis on

21

the right to work where and at what you pleased under a contract of your own making. Wage regulation infringed this individualist principle of the free contract of employment.

The Poor Law was in a somewhat ambiguous position. Elizabethan legislation had made of it something more than a means for relieving destitution and suppressing vagrancy, and its constructive aims suggested an interpretation of social welfare reminiscent of the more primitive, but more genuine, social rights which it had largely superseded. The Elizabethan Poor Law was, after all, one item in a broad programme of economic planning whose general object was, not to create a new social order, but to preserve the existing one with the minimum of essential change. As the pattern of the old order dissolved under the blows of a competitive economy, and the plan disintegrated, the Poor Law was left high and dry as an isolated survival from which the idea of social rights was gradually drained away. But at the very end of the eighteenth century there occurred a final struggle between the old and the new, between the planned (or patterned) society and the competitive economy. And in this battle citizenship was divided against itself; social rights sided with the old and civil with the new.

In his book *Origins of our Time*, Karl Polanyi attributes to the Speenhamland system of poor relief an importance which some readers may find surprising. To him it seems to mark and symbolise the end of an epoch. Through it the old order rallied its retreating forces and delivered a spirited attack into the enemy's country. That, at least,

22

is how I should describe its significance in the history of citizenship. The Speenhamland system offered, in effect, a guaranteed minimum wage and family allowances, combined with the right to work or maintenance. That, even by modern standards, is a substantial body of social rights, going far beyond what one might regard as the proper province of the Poor Law. And it was fully realised by the originators of the scheme that the Poor Law was being invoked to do what wage regulation was no longer able to accomplish. For the Poor Law was the last remains of a system which tried to adjust real income to the social needs and status of the citizen and not solely to the market value of his labour. But this attempt to inject an element of social security into the very structure of the wage system through the instrumentality of the Poor Law was doomed to failure, not only because of its disastrous practical consequences, but also because it was utterly obnoxious to the prevailing spirit of the times.

In this brief episode of our history we see the Poor Law as the aggressive champion of the social rights of citizenship. In the succeeding phase we find the attacker driven back far behind his original position. By the Act of 1834 the Poor Law renounced all claim to trespass on the territory of the wages system, or to interfere with the forces of the free market. It offered relief only to those who, through age or sickness, were incapable of continuing the battle, and to those other weaklings who gave up the struggle, admitted defeat, and cried for mercy. The tentative move towards the concept of social security was reversed. But more than that, the minimal social rights that remained were detached from the status of citizenship. The Poor Law treated the claims of the poor, not as an integral part of the rights of the citizen, but as an alternative to them—as claims which could be met only if the claimants ceased to be citizens in any true sense of the word. For paupers forfeited in practice the civil right of personal liberty, by internment in the workhouse, and they forfeited by law any political rights they might possess. This disability of disfranchisement remained in being until 1918, and the significance of its final removal has, perhaps, not been fully appreciated. The stigma which clung to poor relief expressed the deep feelings of a people who understood that those who accepted relief must cross the road that separated the community of citizens from the outcast company of the destitute.

The Poor Law is not an isolated example of this divorce of social rights from the status of citizenship. The early Factory Acts show the same tendency. Although in fact they led to an improvement of working conditions and a reduction of working hours to the benefit of all employed in the industries to which they applied, they meticulously refrained from giving this protection directly to the adult male—the citizen *par excellence*. And they did so out of respect for his status as a citizen, on the grounds that enforced protective measures curtailed the civil right to conclude a free contract of employment. Protection was confined to women and children, and champions of women's rights were quick to detect the implied insult. Women were protected because they were not citizens. If they wished to enjoy full and responsible citizenship, they

24

must forgo protection. By the end of the nineteenth century such arguments had become obsolete, and the factory code had become one of the pillars in the edifice of social rights.

The history of education shows superficial resemblances to that of factory legislation. In both cases the nineteenth century was, for the most part, a period in which the foundations of social rights were laid, but the principle of social rights as an integral part of the status of citizenship was either expressly denied or not definitely admitted. But there are significant differences. Education, as Marshall recognised when he singled it out as a fit object of State action, is a service of a unique kind. It is easy to say that the recognition of the right of children to be educated does not affect the status of citizenship any more than does the recognition of the right of children to be protected from overwork and dangerous machinery, simply because children, by definition, cannot be citizens. But such a statement is misleading. The education of children has a direct bearing on citizenship, and, when the State guarantees that all children shall be educated, it has the requirements and the nature of citizenship definitely in mind. It is trying to stimulate the growth of citizens in the making. The right to education is a genuine social right of citizenship, because the aim of education during childhood is to shape the future adult. Fundamentally it should be regarded, not as the right of the child to go to school, but as the right of the adult citizen to have been educated. And there is here no conflict with civil rights as interpreted in an age of individualism. For civil rights are designed for use by reasonable and intelligent persons, who have learned to read and write. Education is a necessary prerequisite of civil freedom.

But, by the end of the nineteenth century, elementary education was not only free, it was compulsory. This signal departure from *laissez-faire* could, of course, be justified on the grounds that free choice is a right only for mature minds, that children are naturally subject to discipline, and that parents cannot be trusted to do what is in the best interests of their children. But the principle goes deeper than that. We have here a personal right combined with a public duty to exercise the right. Is the public duty imposed merely for the benefit of the individual—because children cannot fully appreciate their own interests and parents may be unfit to enlighten them? I hardly think that this can be an adequate explanation. It was increasingly recognised, as the nineteenth century wore on, that political democracy needed an educated electorate, and that scientific manufacture needed educated workers and technicians. The duty to improve and civilise oneself is therefore a social duty, and not merely a personal one, because the social health of a society depends upon the civilisation of its members. And a community that enforces this duty has begun to realise that its culture is an organic unity and its civilisation a national heritage. It follows that the growth of public elementary education during the nineteenth century was the first decisive step on the road to the re-establishment of the social rights of citizenship in the twentieth.

When Marshall read his paper to the Cambridge Reform Club, the State was just preparing to shoulder the responsibility he attributed to it when he said that it was 'bound to compel them (the children) and help them to take the first step upwards'. But this would not go far towards realising his ideal of making every man a gentleman, nor was that in the least the intention. And as yet there was little sign of any desire 'to help them, if they will, to make many steps upwards'. The idea was in the air, but it was not a cardinal point of policy. In the early nineties the L.C.C., through its Technical Education Board, instituted a scholarship system which Beatrice Webb obviously regarded as epoch-making. For she wrote of it: 'In its popular aspect this was an educational ladder of unprecedented dimensions. It was, indeed, among educational ladders the most gigantic in extent, the most elaborate in its organisation of "intakes" and promotions, and the most diversified in kinds of excellence selected and in types of training provided that existed anywhere in the world.'[1] The enthusiasm of these words enables us to see how far we have advanced our standards since those days.

3. *The Early Impact of Citizenship on Social Class*

So far my aim has been to trace in outline the development of citizenship in England to the end of the nineteenth century. For this purpose I have divided citizenship into three elements, civil, political and social. I have tried to show that civil rights came first, and were established in something like their modern form before the first Reform Act was passed in 1832. Political rights came

[1] *Our Partnership*, p. 79.

27

next, and their extension was one of the main features of the nineteenth century, although the principle of universal political citizenship was not recognised until 1918. Social rights, on the other hand, sank to vanishing point in the eighteenth and early nineteenth centuries. Their revival began with the development of public elementary education, but it was not until the twentieth century that they attained to equal partnership with the other two elements in citizenship.

I have as yet said nothing about social class, and I should explain here that social class occupies a secondary position in my theme. I do not propose to embark on the long and difficult task of examining its nature and analysing its components. Time would not allow me to do justice to so formidable a subject. My primary concern is with citizenship, and my special interest is in its impact on social inequality. I shall discuss the nature of social class only so far as is necessary for the pursuit of this special interest. I have paused in the narrative at the end of the nineteenth century because I believe that the impact of citizenship on social inequality after that date was fundamentally different from what it had been before it. That statement is not likely to be disputed. It is the exact nature of the difference that is worth exploring. Before going any further, therefore, I shall try to draw some general conclusions about the impact of citizenship on social inequality in the earlier of the two periods.

Citizenship is a status bestowed on those who are full members of a community. All who possess the status are equal with respect to the rights and duties with which the status is endowed. There is no universal principle that determines what those rights and duties shall be, but societies in which citizenship is a developing institution create an image of an ideal citizenship against which achievement can be measured and towards which aspiration can be directed. The urge forward along the path thus plotted is an urge towards a fuller measure of equality, an enrichment of the stuff of which the status is made and an increase in the number of those on whom the status is bestowed. Social class, on the other hand, is a system of inequality. And it too, like citizenship, can be based on a set of ideals, beliefs and values. It is therefore reasonable to expect that the impact of citizenship on social class should take the form of a conflict between opposing principles. If I am right in my contention that citizenship has been a developing institution in England at least since the latter part of the seventeenth century, then it is clear that its growth coincides with the rise of capitalism, which is a system, not of equality, but of inequality. Here is something that needs explaining. How is it that these two opposing principles could grow and flourish side by side in the same soil? What made it possible for them to be reconciled with one another and to become, for a time at least, allies instead of antagonists? The question is a pertinent one, for it is clear that, in the twentieth century, citizenship and the capitalist class system have been at war.

It is at this point that a closer scrutiny of social class becomes necessary. I cannot attempt to examine all its many and varied forms, but there is one broad distinction between two different types of class which is particularly relevant to my argument. In the first of these class is based on a hierarchy of status, and the difference between one class and another is expressed in terms of legal rights and of established customs which have the essential binding character of law. In its extreme form such a system divides a society into a number of distinct, hereditary human species—patricians, plebeians, serfs, slaves and so forth. Class is, as it were, an institution in its own right, and the whole structure has the quality of a plan, in the sense that it is endowed with meaning and purpose and accepted as a natural order. The civilisation at each level is an expression of this meaning and of this natural order, and differences between social levels are not differences in standard of living, because there is no common standard by which they can be measured. Nor are there any rights—at least none of any significance—which all share in common.[1] The impact of citizenship on such a system was bound to be profoundly disturbing, and even destructive. The rights with which the general status of citizenship was invested were extracted from the hierarchical status system of social class, robbing it of its essential substance. The equality implicit in the concept of citizenship, even though limited in content, undermined the inequality of the class system, which was in principle a total inequality. National justice and a law common to all must inevitably weaken and eventually destroy class justice, and personal freedom, as a universal birthright, must drive out serfdom. No

[1] See the admirable characterisation given by R. H. Tawney in *Equality*, pp. 121–2.

subtle argument is needed to show that citizenship is incompatible with medieval feudalism.

Social class of the second type is not so much an institution in its own right as a by-product of other institutions. Although we may still refer to 'social status', we are stretching the term beyond its strict technical meaning when we do so. Class differences are not established and defined by the laws and customs of the society (in the medieval sense of that phrase), but emerge from the interplay of a variety of factors related to the institutions of property and education and the structure of the national economy. Class cultures dwindle to a minimum, so that it becomes possible, though admittedly not wholly satisfactory, to measure the different levels of economic welfare by reference to a common standard of living. The working classes, instead of inheriting a distinctive though simple culture, are provided with a cheap and shoddy imitation of a civilisation that has become national.

It is true that class still functions. Social inequality is regarded as necessary and purposeful. It provides the incentive to effort and designs the distribution of power. But there is no over-all pattern of inequality, in which an appropriate value is attached, *a priori*, to each social level. Inequality therefore, though necessary, may become excessive. As Patrick Colquhoun said, in a much-quoted passage: 'Without a large proportion of poverty there could be no riches, since riches are the offspring of labour, while labour can result only from a state of poverty.... Poverty therefore is a most necessary and indispensable ingredient in society, without which nations and commu-

31

nities could not exist in a state of civilisation.'[1] But Colquhoun, while accepting poverty, deplored 'indigence', or, as we should say, destitution. By 'poverty' he meant the situation of a man who, owing to lack of any economic reserves, is obliged to work, and to work hard, in order to live. By 'indigence' he meant the situation of a family which lacks the minimum necessary for decent living. The system of inequality which allowed the former to exist as a driving force inevitably produced a certain amount of the latter as well. Colquhoun, and other humanitarians, regretted this and sought means to alleviate the suffering it caused. But they did not question the justice of the system of inequality as a whole. It could be argued, in defence of its justice, that, although poverty might be necessary, it was not necessary that any particular family should remain poor, or quite as poor as it was. The more you look on wealth as conclusive proof of merit, the more you incline to regard poverty as evidence of failure—but the penalty for failure may seem to be greater than the offence warrants. In such circumstances it is natural that the more unpleasant features of inequality should be treated, rather irresponsibly, as a nuisance, like the black smoke that used to pour unchecked from our factory chimneys. And so in time, as the social conscience stirs to life, class-abatement, like smoke-abatement, becomes a desirable aim to be pursued as far as is compatible with the continued efficiency of the social machine.

But class-abatement in this form was not an attack on the class system. On the contrary it aimed, often quite

[1] *A Treatise on Indigence* (1806), pp. 7–8.

consciously, at making the class system less vulnerable to attack by alleviating its less defensible consequences. It raised the floor-level in the basement of the social edifice, and perhaps made it rather more hygienic than it was before. But it remained a basement, and the upper stories of the building were unaffected. And the benefits received by the unfortunate did not flow from an enrichment of the status of citizenship. Where they were given officially by the State, this was done by measures which, as I have said, offered alternatives to the rights of citizenship, rather than additions to them. But the major part of the task was left to private charity, and it was the general, though not universal, view of charitable bodies that those who received their help had no personal right to claim it.

Nevertheless it is true that citizenship, even in its early forms, was a principle of equality, and that during this period it was a developing institution. Starting at the point where all men were free and, in theory, capable of enjoying rights, it grew by enriching the body of rights which they were capable of enjoying. But these rights did not conflict with the inequalities of capitalist society; they were, on the contrary, necessary to the maintenance of that particular form of inequality. The explanation lies in the fact that the core of citizenship at this stage was composed of civil rights. And civil rights were indispensable to a competitive market economy. They gave to each man, as part of his individual status, the power to engage as an independent unit in the economic struggle and made it possible to deny to him social protection on the ground that he was equipped with the means to protect himself. Maine's famous dictum that 'the movement of the progressive societies has hitherto been a movement from Status to Contract'[1] expresses a profound truth which has been elaborated, with varying terminology, by many sociologists, but it requires qualification. For both status and contract are present in all but the most primitive societies. Maine himself admitted this when, later in the same book, he wrote that the earliest feudal communities, as contrasted with their archaic predecessors, 'were neither bound together by mere sentiment nor recruited by a fiction. The tie which united them was Contract.'[2] But the contractual element in feudalism co-existed with a class system based on status and, as contract hardened into custom, it helped to perpetuate class status. Custom retained the form of mutual undertakings, but not the reality of a free agreement. Modern contract did not grow out of feudal contract; it marks a new development to whose progress feudalism was an obstacle that had to be swept aside. For modern contract is essentially an agreement between men who are free and equal in status, though not necessarily in power. Status was not eliminated from the social system. Differential status, associated with class, function and family, was replaced by the single uniform status of citizenship, which provided the foundation of equality on which the structure of inequality could be built.

When Maine wrote, this status was clearly an aid, and not a menace, to capitalism and the free-market economy, because it was dominated by civil rights, which confer

[1] *Ancient Law* (1878), p. 170.   [2] *Ib.* p. 365.

the legal capacity to strive for the things one would like to possess but do not guarantee the possession of any of them. A property right is not a right to possess property, but a right to acquire it, if you can, and to protect it, if you can get it. But, if you use these arguments to explain to a pauper that his property rights are the same as those of a millionaire, he will probably accuse you of quibbling. Similarly, the right to freedom of speech has little real substance if, from lack of education, you have nothing to say that is worth saying, and no means of making yourself heard if you say it. But these blatant inequalities are not due to defects in civil rights, but to lack of social rights, and social rights in the mid-nineteenth century were in the doldrums. The Poor Law was an aid, not a menace, to capitalism, because it relieved industry of all social responsibility outside the contract of employment, while sharpening the edge of competition in the labour market. Elementary schooling was also an aid, because it increased the value of the worker without educating him above his station.

But it would be absurd to contend that the civil rights enjoyed in the eighteenth and nineteenth centuries were free from defects, or that they were as egalitarian in practice as they professed to be in principle. Equality before the law did not exist. The right was there, but the remedy might frequently prove to be out of reach. The barriers between rights and remedies were of two kinds: the first arose from class prejudice and partiality, the second from the auto-matic effects of the unequal distribution of wealth, working through the price system. Class prejudice, which un-

3-2

doubtedly coloured the whole administration of justice in the eighteenth century, cannot be eliminated by law, but only by social education and the building of a tradition of impartiality. This is a slow and difficult process, which presupposes a change in the climate of thought throughout the upper ranks of society. But it is a process which I think it is fair to say has been successfully accomplished, in the sense that the tradition of impartiality as between social classes is firmly established in our civil justice. And it is interesting that this should have happened without any fundamental change in the class structure of the legal profession. We have no exact knowledge on this point, but I doubt whether the picture has radically altered since Professor Ginsberg found that the proportion of those admitted to Lincoln's Inn whose fathers were wage-earners had risen from 0·4% in 1904–8 to 1·8% in 1923–27, and that at this latter date nearly 72% were sons of professional men, high-ranking business men and gentlemen.[1] The decline of class prejudice as a barrier to the full enjoyment of rights is, therefore, due less to the dilution of class monopoly in the legal profession than to the spread in all classes of a more humane and realistic sense of social equality.

It is interesting to compare with this the corresponding development in the field of political rights. Here too class prejudice, expressed through the intimidation of the lower classes by the upper, prevented the free exercise of the right to vote by the newly enfranchised. In this case a practical remedy was available, in the secret ballot. But

[1] *Studies in Sociology*, p. 171.

that was not enough. Social education, and a change of mental climate, were needed as well. And, even when voters felt free from undue influence, it still took some time to break down the idea, prevalent in the working as well as other classes, that the representatives of the people, and still more the members of the government, should be drawn from among the élites who were born, bred and educated for leadership. Class monopoly in politics, unlike class monopoly in law, has definitely been overthrown. Thus, in these two fields, the same goal has been reached by rather different paths.

The removal of the second obstacle, the effects of the unequal distribution of wealth, was technically a simple matter in the case of political rights, because it costs little or nothing to register a vote. Nevertheless, wealth can be used to influence an election, and a series of measures was adopted to reduce this influence. The earlier ones, which go back to the seventeenth century, were directed against bribery and corruption, but the later ones, especially from 1883 onwards, had the wider aim of limiting election expenses in general, in order that candidates of unequal wealth might fight on more or less equal terms. The need for such equalising measures has now greatly diminished, since working-class candidates can get financial support from party and other funds. Restrictions which prevent competitive extravagance are, therefore, probably welcomed by all. It remained to open the House of Commons to men of all classes, regardless of wealth, first by abolishing the property qualification for members, and then by introducing payment of members in 1911.

It has proved far more difficult to achieve similar results in the field of civil rights, because litigation, unlike voting, is very expensive. Court fees are not high, but counsel's fees and solicitor's charges may mount up to very large sums indeed. Since a legal action takes the form of a contest, each party feels that his chances of winning will be improved if he secures the services of better champions than those employed on the other side. There is, of course, some truth in this, but not as much as is popularly believed. But the effect in litigation, as in elections, is to introduce an element of competitive extravagance which makes it difficult to estimate in advance what the costs of an action will amount to. In addition, our system by which costs are normally awarded to the winner increases the risk and the uncertainty. A man of limited means, knowing that, if he loses, he will have to pay his opponent's costs (after they have been pruned by the Taxing Master) as well as his own, may easily be frightened into accepting an unsatisfactory settlement, especially if his opponent is wealthy enough not to be bothered by any such considerations. And even if he wins, the taxed costs he recovers will usually be less than his actual expenditure, and often considerably less. So that, if he has been induced to fight his case expensively, the victory may not be worth the price paid.

What, then, has been done to remove these barriers to the full and equal exercise of civil rights? Only one thing of real substance, the establishment in 1846 of the County Courts to provide cheap justice for the common people. This important innovation has had a profound and beneficial effect on our legal system, and done much to develop a proper sense of the importance of the case brought by the small man—which is often a very big case by his standards. But County Court costs are not negligible, and the jurisdiction of the County Courts is limited. The second major step taken was the development of a poor person's procedure, under which a small fraction of the poorer members of the community could sue *in forma pauperis*, practically free of all cost, being assisted by the gratuitous and voluntary services of the legal profession. But, as the income limit was extremely low (£2 a week since 1919), and the procedure did not apply in the County Courts, it has had little effect except in matrimonial causes. The supplementary service of free legal advice was, until recently, provided by the unaided efforts of voluntary bodies. But the problem has not been overlooked, nor the reality of the defects in our system denied. It has attracted increasing attention during the last hundred years. The machinery of the Royal Commission and the Committee has been used repeatedly, and some reforms of procedure have resulted. Two such Committees are at work now, but it would be most improper for me to make any reference to their deliberations.[1] A third, which started earlier, issued a report on which is based the Legal Aid and Advice Bill laid before parliament just three months ago.[2] This is a bold measure, going far beyond

[1] The Austin Jones Committee on County Court Procedure and the Evershed Committee on Supreme Court Practice and Procedure. The report of the former and an interim report of the latter have since been published.

[2] The Rushcliffe Committee on Legal Aid and Legal Advice in England and Wales.

anything previously attempted for the assistance of the poorer litigants, and I shall have more to say about it later on.

It is apparent from the events I have briefly narrated that there developed, in the latter part of the nineteenth century, a growing interest in equality as a principle of social justice and an appreciation of the fact that the formal recognition of an equal capacity for rights was not enough. In theory even the complete removal of all the barriers that separated civil rights from their remedies would not have interfered with the principles or the class structure of the capitalist system. It would, in fact, have created a situation which many supporters of the competitive market economy falsely assumed to be already in existence. But in practice the attitude of mind which inspired the efforts to remove these barriers grew out of a conception of equality which overstepped these narrow limits, the conception of equal social worth, not merely of equal natural rights. Thus although citizenship, even by the end of the nineteenth century, had done little to reduce social inequality, it had helped to guide progress into the path which led directly to the egalitarian policies of the twentieth century.

It also had an integrating effect, or, at least, was an important ingredient in an integrating process. In a passage I quoted just now Maine spoke of pre-feudal societies as bound together by a sentiment and recruited by a fiction. He was referring to kinship, or the fiction of common descent. Citizenship requires a bond of a different kind, a direct sense of community membership

40

based on loyalty to a civilisation which is a common possession. It is a loyalty of free men endowed with rights and protected by a common law. Its growth is stimulated both by the struggle to win those rights and by their enjoyment when won. We see this clearly in the eighteenth century, which saw the birth, not only of modern civil rights, but also of modern national consciousness. The familiar instruments of modern democracy were fashioned by the upper classes and then handed down, step by step, to the lower: political journalism for the intelligentsia was followed by newspapers for all who could read, public meetings, propaganda campaigns, and associations for the furtherance of public causes. Repressive measures and taxes were quite unable to stop the flood. And with it came a patriotic nationalism, expressing the unity underlying these controversial outbursts. How deep or widespread this was it is difficult to say, but there can be no doubt about the vigour of its outward manifestation. We still use those typically eighteenth-century songs, 'God Save the King' and 'Rule Britannia', but we omit the passages which would offend our modern, and more modest, sensibilities. This jingo patriotism, and the 'popular and parliamentary agitation' which Temperley found to be 'the main factor in causing the war' of Jenkins's ear,[1] were new phenomena in which can be recognised the first small trickle which grew into the broad stream of the national war efforts of the twentieth century.

This growing national consciousness, this awakening

[1] C. Grant Robertson, *England under the Hanoverians*, p. 491.

public opinion, and these first stirrings of a sense of community membership and common heritage did not have any material effect on class structure and social inequality for the simple and obvious reason that, even at the end of the nineteenth century, the mass of the working people did not wield effective political power. By that time the franchise was fairly wide, but those who had recently received the vote had not yet learned how to use it. The political rights of citizenship, unlike the civil rights, were full of potential danger to the capitalist system, although those who were cautiously extending them down the social scale probably did not realise quite how great the danger was. They could hardly be expected to foresee what vast changes could be brought about by the peaceful use of political power, without a violent and bloody revolution. The Planned Society and the Welfare State had not yet risen over the horizon or come within the view of the practical politician. The foundations of the market economy and the contractual system seemed strong enough to stand against any probable assault. In fact, there were some grounds for expecting that the working classes, as they became educated, would accept the basic principles of the system and be content to rely for their protection and progress on the civil rights of citizenship, which contained no obvious menace to competitive capitalism. Such a view was encouraged by the fact that one of the main achievements of political power in the later nineteenth century was the recognition of the right of collective bargaining. This meant that social progress was being sought by strengthening civil rights, not by creating social rights; through the use of contract in the open market, not through a minimum wage and social security.

But this interpretation underrates the significance of this extension of civil rights in the economic sphere. For civil rights were in origin intensely individual, and that is why they harmonised with the individualistic phase of capitalism. By the device of incorporation groups were enabled to act legally as individuals. This important development did not go unchallenged, and limited liability was widely denounced as an infringement of individual responsibility. But the position of trade unions was even more anomalous, because they did not seek or obtain incorporation. They can, therefore, exercise vital civil rights collectively on behalf of their members without formal collective responsibility, while the individual responsibility of the workers in relation to contract is largely unenforceable. These civil rights became, for the workers, an instrument for raising their social and economic status, that is to say, for establishing the claim that they, as citizens, were entitled to certain social rights. But the normal method of establishing social rights is by the exercise of political power, for social rights imply an absolute right to a certain standard of civilisation which is conditional only on the discharge of the general duties of citizenship. Their content does not depend on the economic value of the individual claimant. There is therefore a significant difference between a genuine collective bargain through which economic forces in a free market seek to achieve equilibrium and the use of collective civil

43

rights to assert basic claims to the elements of social justice. Thus the acceptance of collective bargaining was not simply a natural extension of civil rights; it represented the transfer of an important process from the political to the civil sphere of citizenship. But 'transfer' is, perhaps, a misleading term, for at the time when this happened the workers either did not possess, or had not yet learned to use, the political right of the franchise. Since then they have obtained and made full use of that right. Trade unionism has, therefore, created a secondary system of industrial citizenship parallel with and supplementary to the system of political citizenship.

It is interesting to compare this development with the history of parliamentary representation. In the early parliaments, says Pollard, 'representation was nowise regarded as a means of expressing individual right or forwarding individual interests. It was communities, not individuals, who were represented.'[1] And, looking at the position on the eve of the Reform Act of 1918, he added: 'Parliament, instead of representing communities or families, is coming to represent nothing but individuals.'[2] A system of manhood and womanhood suffrage treats the vote as the voice of the individual. Political parties organise these voices for group action, but they do so nationally and not on the basis of function, locality or interest. In the case of civil rights the movement has been in the opposite direction, not from the representation of communities to that of individuals, but from the representation of individuals to that of communities. And

[1] *The Evolution of Parliament*, p. 155.   [2] *Ib.* p. 165.

44

Pollard makes another point. It was a characteristic of the early parliamentary system, he says, that the representatives were those who had the time, the means and the inclination to do the job. Election by a majority of votes and strict accountability to the electors was not essential. Constituencies did not instruct their members, and election promises were unknown. Members 'were elected to bind their constituents, and not to be bound by them.'[1] It is not too fanciful to suggest that some of these features are reproduced in modern trade unions, though, of course, with many profound differences. One of these is that trade union officials do not undertake an onerous unpaid job, but enter on a remunerative career. This remark is not meant to be offensive, and, indeed, it would hardly be seemly for a university professor to criticise a public institution on the ground that its affairs are managed largely by its salaried employees.

All that I have said so far has been by way of introduction to my main task. I have not tried to put before you new facts culled by laborious research. The limit of my ambition has been to regroup familiar facts in a pattern which may make them appear to some of you in a new light. I thought it necessary to do this in order to prepare the ground for the more difficult, speculative and controversial study of the contemporary scene, in which the leading role is played by the social rights of citizenship. It is to the impact of these on social class that I must now turn my attention.

[1] *Ib.* p. 152.

45

4. *Social Rights in the Twentieth Century*

The period of which I have hitherto been speaking was one during which the growth of citizenship, substantial and impressive though it was, had little direct effect on social inequality. Civil rights gave legal powers whose use was drastically curtailed by class prejudice and lack of economic opportunity. Political rights gave potential power whose exercise demanded experience, organisation, and a change of ideas as to the proper functions of government. All these took time to develop. Social rights were at a minimum and were not woven into the fabric of citizenship. The common purpose of statutory and voluntary effort was to abate the nuisance of poverty without disturbing the pattern of inequality of which poverty was the most obviously unpleasant consequence.

A new period opened at the end of the nineteenth century, conveniently marked by Booth's survey of Life and Labour of the People in London and the Royal Commission on the Aged Poor. It saw the first big advance in social rights, and this involved significant changes in the egalitarian principle as expressed in citizenship. But there were other forces at work as well. A rise of money incomes unevenly distributed over the social classes altered the economic distance which separated these classes from one another, diminishing the gap between skilled and unskilled labour and between skilled labour and non-manual workers, while the steady increase in small savings blurred the class distinction between the capitalist and the propertyless proletarian. Secondly, a system of direct taxation, ever more steeply graduated, compressed the whole scale of disposable incomes. Thirdly, mass production for the home market and a growing interest on the part of industry in the needs and tastes of the common people enabled the less well-to-do to enjoy a material civilisation which differed less markedly in quality from that of the rich than it had ever done before. All this profoundly altered the setting in which the progress of citizenship took place. Social integration spread from the sphere of sentiment and patriotism into that of material enjoyment. The components of a civilised and cultured life, formerly the monopoly of the few, were brought progressively within reach of the many, who were encouraged thereby to stretch out their hands towards those that still eluded their grasp. The diminution of inequality strengthened the demand for its abolition, at least with regard to the essentials of social welfare.

These aspirations have in part been met by incorporating social rights in the status of citizenship and thus creating a universal right to real income which is not proportionate to the market value of the claimant. Class-abatement is still the aim of social rights, but it has acquired a new meaning. It is no longer merely an attempt to abate the obvious nuisance of destitution in the lowest ranks of society. It has assumed the guise of action modifying the whole pattern of social inequality. It is no longer content to raise the floor-level in the basement of the social edifice, leaving the superstructure as it was. It has begun to remodel the whole building, and it might even end by converting a sky-scraper into a bungalow.

47

It is therefore important to consider whether any such ultimate aim is implicit in the nature of this development, or whether, as I put it at the outset, there are natural limits to the contemporary drive towards greater social and economic equality. To answer this question I must survey and analyse the social services of the twentieth century.

I said earlier that the attempts made to remove the barriers between civil rights and their remedies gave evidence of a new attitude towards the problem of equality. I can therefore conveniently begin my survey by looking at the latest example of such an attempt, the Legal Aid and Advice Bill, which offers a social service designed to strengthen the civil right of the citizen to settle his disputes in a court of law. It also brings us face to face at once with one of the major issues of our problem, the possibility of combining in one system the two principles of social justice and market price. The State is not prepared to make the administration of justice free for all. One reason for this—though not, of course, the only one—is that costs perform a useful function by discouraging frivolous litigation and encouraging the acceptance of reasonable settlements. If all actions which are started went to trial, the machinery of justice would break down. Also, the amount that it is appropriate to spend on a case depends largely on what it is worth to the parties, and of this, it is argued, they themselves are the only judges. It is very different in a health service, where the seriousness of the disease and the nature of the treatment required can be objectively assessed with very little reference to the importance the patient attaches to it. Nevertheless, though

48

some payment is demanded, it must not take a form which deprives the litigant of his right to justice or puts him at a disadvantage *vis-à-vis* his opponent.

The main provisions of the scheme are as follows. The service will be confined to an economic class—those whose disposable income and capital do not exceed £420 and £500 respectively.[1] 'Disposable' means the balance after considerable deductions have been allowed for dependants, rent, ownership of house and tools, and so forth. The maximum contributable by the litigant towards his own costs is limited to half the excess of his disposable income over £156 plus the excess of his disposable capital above £75. His liability towards the costs of the other side, if he loses, is entirely in the discretion of the court. He will have the professional assistance of solicitor and counsel drawn from a panel of volunteers, and they will be remunerated for their services, in the High Court (and above) at rates 15% below what the Taxing Master would regard as reasonable in the free market, and in the County Court according to uniform scales not yet fixed.

The scheme, it will be seen, makes use of the principles of the income limit and the means test, which have just been abandoned in the other major social services. And the means test will be applied, or the maximum contribution assessed, by the National Assistance Board, whose officers, in addition to making the allowances prescribed

---

[1] Where disposable capital exceeds £500, legal aid may still be granted, at the discretion of the local committee, if disposable income does not exceed £420.

in the regulations, 'will have general discretionary powers to enable them to deduct from income any sums which they normally disregard in dealing with an application for assistance under the National Assistance Act, 1948'.[1] It will be interesting to see whether this link with the old Poor Law will make Legal Aid unsavoury to many of those entitled to avail themselves of it, who will include persons with gross incomes up to £600 or £700 a year. But, quite apart from the agents employed to enforce it, the reason for introducing a means test is clear. The price payable for the service of the court and of the legal profession plays a useful part by testing the urgency of the demand. It is, therefore, to be retained. But the impact of price on demand is to be made less unequal by adjusting the bill to the income out of which it must be met. The method of adjustment resembles the operation of a progressive tax. If we consider income only, and ignore capital, we see that a man with a disposable income of £200 would be liable to contribute £22, or 11% of that income, and a man with a disposable income of £420 would have a maximum contribution of £132, or over 31% of that income.

A system of this kind may work quite well (assuming the scale of adjustment to be satisfactory) provided the market price of the service is a reasonable one for the smallest income that does not qualify for assistance. Then the price scale can taper down from this pivotal point until it vanishes where the income is too small to pay anything. No awkward gap will appear at the top between

[1] Cmd. 7563: Summary of the Proposed New Service, p. 7, para. 17.

the assisted and the unassisted. The method is in use for State scholarships to universities. The cost to be met in this case is the standardised figure for maintenance plus fees. Deductions are made from the gross income of the parents on lines similar to those proposed for Legal Aid, except that income tax is not deducted. The resulting figure is known as the 'scale income'. This is applied to a table which shows the parental contribution at each point on the scale. Scale incomes up to £600 pay nothing, and the ceiling above which parents must pay the full costs, without subsidy, is £1500. A Working Party has recently recommended that the ceiling should be raised 'to at least £2000' (before tax),[1] which is a fairly generous poverty line for a social service. It is not unreasonable to assume that, at that income level, the market cost of a university education can be met by the family without undue hardship.

The Legal Aid scheme will probably work in much the same way for County Court cases, where costs are moderate. Those with incomes at the top of the scale will not normally receive any subsidy towards their own costs, even if they lose their case. The contribution they can be called on to make out of their own funds will usually be enough to cover them. They will thus be in the same position as those just outside the scheme, and no awkward gap will appear. Litigants coming within the scheme, will, however, get professional legal assistance at a controlled and

[1] Ministry of Education: *Report of the Working Party on University Awards*, 1948, para. 60. The general account of the present system is taken from the same source.

reduced price, and that is in itself a valuable privilege. But in a heavy High Court case the maximum contribution of the man at the top of the scale would be far from sufficient to meet his own costs if he was defeated. His liability under the scheme could, therefore, be many times less than that of a man, just outside the scheme, who fought and lost an identical action. In such cases the gap may be very noticeable, and this is particularly serious in litigation, which takes the form of a contest. The contest may be between an assisted litigant and an unassisted one, and they will be fighting under different rules. One will be protected by the principle of social justice, while the other is left to the mercy of the market and the ordinary obligations imposed by contract and the rules of the court. A measure of class-abatement may, in some cases, create a form of class privilege. Whether this will happen depends largely on the content of regulations which have not yet been issued, and on the way in which the court uses its discretion in awarding costs against assisted litigants who lose their actions.

This particular difficulty could be overcome if the system were made universal, or nearly so, by carrying the scale of maximum contributions up to much higher income levels. In other words, the means test could be preserved, but the income limit dropped. But this would mean bringing all, or practically all, legal practitioners into the scheme, and subjecting them to controlled prices for their services. It would amount almost to the nationalisation of the profession, so far as litigation is concerned, or so it would probably appear to the barristers, whose profession is inspired by a strong spirit of individualism. And the disappearance of private practice would deprive the Taxing Masters of a standard by which to fix the controlled price.

I have chosen this example to illustrate some of the difficulties that arise when one tries to combine the principles of social equality and the price system. Differential price adjustment by scale to different incomes is one method of doing this. It was widely used by doctors and hospitals until the National Health Service made this unnecessary. It frees real income, in certain forms, from its dependence on money income. If the principle were universally applied, differences in money income would become meaningless. The same result could be achieved by making all gross incomes equal, or by reducing unequal gross incomes to equal net incomes by taxation. Both processes have been going on, up to a point. Both are checked by the need to preserve differential incomes as a source of economic incentive. But, when different methods of doing much the same thing are combined, it may be possible to carry the process much further without upsetting the economic machine, because their various consequences are not easily added together, and the total effect may escape notice in the general confusion. And we must remember that gross money incomes provide the measuring-rod by which we traditionally assess social and economic achievement and prestige. Even if they lost all meaning in terms of real income, they might still function, like orders and decorations, as spurs to effort and badges of success.

But I must return to my survey of the social services. The most familiar principle in use is not, of course, the scaled price (which I have just been discussing), but the guaranteed minimum. The State guarantees a minimum supply of certain essential goods and services (such as medical attention and supplies, shelter, and education) or a minimum money income available to be spent on essentials—as in the case of Old Age Pensions, insurance benefits, and family allowances. Anyone able to exceed the guaranteed minimum out of his own resources is at liberty to do so. Such a system looks, on the face of it, like a more generous version of class-abatement in its original form. It raises the floor-level at the bottom, but does not automatically flatten the superstructure. But its effects need closer examination.

The degree of equalisation achieved depends on four things—whether the benefit is offered to all or to a limited class; whether it takes the form of money payment or service rendered; whether the minimum is high or low; and how the money to pay for the benefit is raised. Cash benefits subject to income limit and means test had a simple and obvious equalising effect. They achieved class-abatement in the early and limited sense of the term. The aim was to ensure that all citizens should attain at least to the prescribed minimum, either by their own resources or with assistance if they could not do it without. The benefit was given only to those who needed it, and thus inequalities at the bottom of the scale were ironed out. The system operated in its simplest and most unadulterated form in the case of the Poor Law and Old Age Pensions.

But economic equalisation might be accompanied by psychological class discrimination. The stigma which attached to the Poor Law made 'pauper' a derogatory term defining a class. 'Old Age Pensioner' may have had a little of the same flavour, but without the taint of shame.

The general effect of social insurance, when confined to an income group, was similar. It differed in that there was no means test. Contribution gave a right to benefit. But, broadly speaking, the income of the group was raised by the excess of benefits over total expenditure by the group in contributions and additional taxes, and the income gap between this group and those above it was thereby reduced. The exact effect is hard to estimate, because of the wide range of incomes within the group and the varying incidence of the risks covered. When the scheme was extended to all, this gap was reopened, though again we have to take account of the combined effects of the regressive flat-rate levy and the, in part, progressive taxation which contributed to the financing of the scheme. Nothing will induce me to embark on a discussion of this problem. But a total scheme is less specifically class-abating in a purely economic sense than a limited one, and social insurance is less so than a means-test service. Flat-rate benefits do not reduce the gaps between different incomes. Their equalising effect depends on the fact that they make a bigger percentage addition to small incomes than to large. And, even though the concept of diminishing marginal utility (if one may still refer to it) can strictly be applied only to the rising income of one unchanging individual, that remains a matter of some significance. When a free service, as in the case of health, is extended from a limited income group to the whole population, the direct effect is in part to increase the inequality of disposable incomes, again subject to modification by the incidence of taxes. For members of the middle classes, who used to pay their doctors, find this part of their income released for expenditure on other things.

I have been skating gingerly over this very thin ice in order to make one point. The extension of the social services is not primarily a means of equalising incomes. In some cases it may, in others it may not. The question is relatively unimportant; it belongs to a different department of social policy. What matters is that there is a general enrichment of the concrete substance of civilised life, a general reduction of risk and insecurity, an equalisation between the more and the less fortunate at all levels—between the healthy and the sick, the employed and the unemployed, the old and the active, the bachelor and the father of a large family. Equalisation is not so much between classes as between individuals within a population which is now treated for this purpose as though it were one class. Equality of status is more important than equality of income.

Even when benefits are paid in cash, this class fusion is outwardly expressed in the form of a new common experience. All learn what it means to have an insurance card that must be regularly stamped (by somebody), or to collect children's allowances or pensions from the post office. But where the benefit takes the form of a service, the qualitative element enters into the benefit itself, and not only into the process by which it is obtained. The extension of such services can therefore have a profound effect on the qualitative aspects of social differentiation. The old elementary schools, though open to all, were used by a social class (admittedly a very large and varied one) for which no other kind of education was available. Its members were brought up in segregation from the higher classes and under influences which set their stamp on the children subjected to them. 'Ex-elementary school boy' became a label which a man might carry through life, and it pointed to a distinction which was real, and not merely conventional, in character. For a divided educational system, by promoting both intra-class similarity and inter-class difference, gave emphasis and precision to a criterion of social distance. As Professor Tawney has said, translating the views of educationalists into his own inimitable prose: 'The intrusion into educational organisation of the vulgarities of the class system is an irrelevance as mischievous in effect as it is odious in conception.'[1] The limited service was class-making at the same time as it was class-abating. To-day the segregation still takes place, but subsequent education, available to all, makes it possible for a re-sorting to take place. I shall have to consider in a moment whether class intrudes in a different way into this re-sorting.

Similarly the early health service added 'panel patient' to our vocabulary of social class, and many members of the middle classes are now learning exactly what the term

[1] *Secondary Education for all*, p. 64.

57

signifies. But the extension of the service has reduced the social importance of the distinction. The common experience offered by a general health service embraces all but a small minority at the top and spreads across the important class barriers in the middle ranks of the hierarchy. At the same time the guaranteed minimum has been raised to such a height that the term 'minimum' becomes a misnomer. The intention, at least, is to make it approximate so nearly to the reasonable maximum that the extras which the rich are still able to buy will be no more than frills and luxuries. The provided service, not the purchased service, becomes the norm of social welfare. Some people think that, in such circumstances, the independent sector cannot survive for long. If it disappears, the skyscraper will have been converted into a bungalow. If the present system continues and attains its ideals, the result might be described as a bungalow surmounted by an architecturally insignificant turret.

Benefits in the form of a service have this further characteristic that the rights of the citizen cannot be precisely defined. The qualitative element is too great. A modicum of legally enforceable rights may be granted, but what matters to the citizen is the superstructure of legitimate expectations. It may be fairly easy to enable every child below a certain age to spend the required number of hours in school. It is much harder to satisfy the legitimate expectation that the education should be given by trained teachers in classes of moderate size. It may be possible for every citizen who wishes it to be registered with a doctor. It is much harder to ensure that his ailments will be properly cared for. And so we find that legislation, instead of being the decisive step that puts policy into immediate effect, acquires more and more the character of a declaration of policy that it is hoped to put into effect some day. We think at once of County Colleges and Health Centres. The rate of progress depends on the magnitude of the national resources and their distribution between competing claims. Nor can the State easily foresee what it will cost to fulfil its obligations, for, as the standard expected of the service rises—as it inevitably must in a progressive society—the obligations automatically get heavier. The target is perpetually moving forward, and the State may never be able to get quite within range of it. It follows that individual rights must be subordinated to national plans.

Expectations officially recognised as legitimate are not claims that must be met in each case when presented. They become, as it were, details in a design for community living. The obligation of the State is towards society as a whole, whose remedy in case of default lies in parliament or a local council, instead of to individual citizens, whose remedy lies in a court of law, or at least in a quasi-judicial tribunal. The maintenance of a fair balance between these collective and individual elements in social rights is a matter of vital importance to the democratic socialist State.

The point I have just made is clearest in the case of housing. Here the tenure of existing dwellings has been protected by firm legal rights, enforceable in a court of law. The system has become very complicated, because it has grown piecemeal, and it cannot be maintained that the benefits are equally distributed in proportion to real need. But the basic right of the individual citizen to have a dwelling at all is minimal. He can claim no more than a roof over his head, and his claim can be met, as we have seen in recent years, by a shake-down in a disused cinema converted into a rest centre. Nevertheless, the general obligation of the State towards society collectively with regard to housing is one of the heaviest it has to bear. Public policy has unequivocally given the citizen a legitimate expectation of a home fit for a family to live in, and the promise is not now confined to heroes. It is true that, in dealing with individual claims, authorities work as far as possible on a priority scale of needs. But, when a slum is being cleared, an old city remodelled, or a new town planned, individual claims must be subordinated to the general programme of social advance. An element of chance, and therefore of inequality, enters. One family may be moved ahead of its turn into a model dwelling, because it is part of a community due for early treatment. A second will have to wait, although its physical conditions may be worse than those of the first. As the work goes on, though in many places inequalities vanish, in others they become more apparent. Let me give you one small example of this. In the town of Middlesbrough, part of the population of a blighted area had been moved to a new housing estate. It was found that, among the children living on this estate, one in eight of those who competed for places in secondary schools were successful. Among the section of the same original population that had been left behind the proportion was one in one hundred and fifty-four.[1] The contrast is so staggering that one hesitates to offer any precise explanation of it, but it remains a striking example of inequality between individuals appearing as the interim result of the progressive satisfaction of collective social rights. Eventually, when the housing programme has been completed, such inequalities should disappear.

There is another aspect of housing policy which, I believe, implies the intrusion of a new element into the rights of citizenship. It comes into play when the design for living, to which I have said individual rights must be subordinated, is not limited to one section at the bottom of the social scale nor to one particular type of need, but covers the general aspects of the life of a whole community. Town-planning is total planning in this sense. Not only does it treat the community as a whole, but it affects and must take account of all social activities, customs and interests. It aims at creating new physical environments which will actively foster the growth of new human societies. It must decide what these societies are to be like, and try to provide for all the major diversities which they ought to contain. Town-planners are fond of talking about a 'balanced community' as their objective. This means a society that contains a proper mixture of all social classes, as well as of age and sex groups, occupations and so forth. They do not want to build working-class neighbourhoods and middle-class neighbourhoods, but they do propose to build working-class houses and middle-

[1] Ruth Glass, *The Social Background of a Plan*, p. 129.

class houses. Their aim is not a classless society, but a society in which class differences are legitimate in terms of social justice, and in which, therefore, the classes co-operate more closely than at present to the common benefit of all. When a planning authority decides that it needs a larger middle-class element in its town (as it very often does) and makes designs to meet its needs and fit its standards, it is not, like a speculative builder, merely responding to a commercial demand. It must re-interpret the demand in harmony with its total plan and then give it the sanction of its authority as the responsible organ of a community of citizens. The middle-class man can then say, not 'I will come if you pay the price I feel strong enough to demand', but 'If you want me as a citizen, you must give me the status which is due as of right to the kind of citizen I am.' This is one example of the way in which citizenship is itself becoming the architect of social inequality.

The second, and more important, example is in the field of education, which also illustrates my earlier point about the balance between individual and collective social rights. In the first phase of our public education, rights were minimal and equal. But, as we have observed, a duty was attached to the right, not merely because the citizen has a duty to himself, as well as a right, to develop all that is in him—a duty which neither the child nor the parent may fully appreciate—but because society recognised that it needed an educated population. In fact the nineteenth century has been accused of regarding elementary education solely as a means of providing capitalist employers with more valuable workers, and higher education merely as an instrument to increase the power of the nation to compete with its industrial rivals. And you may have noticed that recent studies of educational opportunity in the pre-war years have been concerned to reveal the magnitude of social waste quite as much as to protest against the frustration of natural human rights.

In the second phase of our educational history, which began in 1902, the educational ladder was officially accepted as an important, though still small, part of the system. But the balance between collective and individual rights remained much the same. The State decided what it could afford to spend on free secondary and higher education, and the children competed for the limited number of places provided. There was no pretence that all who could benefit from more advanced education would get it, and there was no recognition of any absolute natural right to be educated according to one's capacities. But in the third phase, which started in 1944, individual rights have ostensibly been given priority. Competition for scarce places is to be replaced by selection and distribution into appropriate places, sufficient in number to accommodate all, at least at the secondary school level. In the Act of 1944 there is a passage which says that the supply of secondary schools will not be considered adequate unless they 'afford for all pupils opportunities for education offering such variety of instruction and training as may be desirable in view of their different ages, abilities and aptitudes.' Respect for individual rights could hardly be more strongly expressed. Yet I wonder whether it will work out like that in practice.

If it were possible for the school system to treat the pupil entirely as an end in himself, and to regard education as giving him something whose value he could enjoy to the full whatever his station in after-life, then it might be possible to mould the educational plan to the shape demanded by individual needs, regardless of any other considerations. But, as we all know, education to-day is closely linked with occupation, and one, at least, of the values the pupil expects to get from it is a qualification for employment at an appropriate level. Unless great changes take place, it seems likely that the educational plan will be adjusted to occupational demand. The proportion between Grammar, Technical and Modern Secondary Schools cannot well be fixed without reference to the proportion between jobs of corresponding grades. And a balance between the two systems may have to be sought in justice to the pupil himself. For if a boy who is given a Grammar School education can then get nothing but a Modern School job, he will cherish a grievance and feel that he has been cheated. It is highly desirable that this attitude should change, so that a boy in such circumstances will be grateful for his education and not resentful at his job. But to accomplish such a change is no easy task.

I see no signs of any relaxation of the bonds that tie education to occupation. On the contrary, they appear to be growing stronger. Great and increasing respect is paid to certificates, matriculation, degrees and diplomas as qualifications for employment, and their freshness does not fade with the passage of the years. A man of forty may be judged by his performance in an examination taken at

64

the age of fifteen. The ticket obtained on leaving school or college is for a life journey. The man with a third-class ticket who later feels entitled to claim a seat in a first-class carriage will not be admitted, even if he is prepared to pay the difference. That would not be fair to the others. He must go back to the start and re-book, by passing the prescribed examination. And it is unlikely that the State will offer to pay his return fare. This is not, of course, true of the whole field of employment, but it is a fair description of a large and significant part of it, whose extension is being constantly advocated. I have, for instance, recently read an article in which it is urged that every aspirant to an administrative or managerial post in business should be required to qualify 'by passing the matriculation or equivalent examination'.[1] This development is partly the result of the systematisation of techniques in more and more professional, semi-professional and skilled occupations, though I must confess that some of the claims of so-called professional bodies to exclusive possession of esoteric skill and knowledge appear to me to be rather thin. But it is also fostered by the refinement of the selective process within the educational system itself. The more confident the claim of education to be able to sift human material during the early years of life, the more is mobility concentrated within those years, and consequently limited thereafter.

The right of the citizen in this process of selection and mobility is the right to equality of opportunity. Its aim is to eliminate hereditary privilege. In essence it is the equal right to display and develop differences, or

[1] J. A. Bowie, in *Industry* (January 1949), p. 17.

inequalities; the equal right to be recognised as unequal. In the early stages of the establishment of such a system the major effect is, of course, to reveal hidden equalities— to enable the poor boy to show that he is as good as the rich boy. But the final outcome is a structure of unequal status fairly apportioned to unequal abilities. The process is sometimes associated with ideas of *laissez-faire* individualism, but within the educational system it is a matter, not of *laissez-faire*, but of planning. The process through which abilities are revealed, the influences to which they are subjected, the tests by which they are measured, and the rights given as a result of the tests are all planned. Equality of opportunity is offered to all children entering the primary schools, but at an early age they are usually divided into three streams—the best, the average and the backward. Already opportunity is becoming unequal, and the children's range of chances limited. About the age of eleven they are tested again, probably by a team of teachers, examiners and psychologists. None of these is infallible, but perhaps sometimes three wrongs may make a right. Classification follows for distribution into the three types of secondary school. Opportunity becomes still more unequal, and the chance of further education has already been limited to a select few. Some of these, after being tested again, will go on to receive it. In the end the jumble of mixed seed originally put into the machine emerges in neatly labelled packets ready to be sown in the appropriate gardens.

I have deliberately couched this description in the language of cynicism in order to bring out the point that, however genuine may be the desire of the educational authorities to offer enough variety to satisfy all individual needs, they must, in a mass service of this kind, proceed by repeated classification into groups, and this is followed at each stage by assimilation within each group and differentiation between groups. That is precisely the way in which social classes in a fluid society have always taken shape. Differences within each class are ignored as irrelevant; differences between classes are given exaggerated significance. Thus qualities which are in reality strung out along a continuous scale are made to create a hierarchy of groups, each with its special character and status. The main features of the system are inevitable, and its advantages, in particular the elimination of inherited privilege, far outweigh its incidental defects. The latter can be attacked and kept within bounds by giving as much opportunity as possible for second thoughts about classification, both in the educational system itself and in after-life.

The conclusion of importance to my argument is that, through education in its relations with occupational structure, citizenship operates as an instrument of social stratification. There is no reason to deplore this, but we should be aware of its consequences. The status acquired by education is carried out into the world bearing the stamp of legitimacy, because it has been conferred by an institution designed to give the citizen his just rights. That which the market offers can be measured against that which the status claims. If a large discrepancy appears, the ensuing attempts to eliminate it will take the form, not of a bargain about economic value, but of a debate about social rights. And it may be that there is already a serious discrepancy between the expectations of those who reach the middle grades in education and the status of the non-manual jobs for which they are normally destined.

I said earlier that in the twentieth century citizenship and the capitalist class system have been at war. Perhaps the phrase is rather too strong, but it is quite clear that the former has imposed modifications on the latter. But we should not be justified in assuming that, although status is a principle that conflicts with contract, the stratified status system which is creeping into citizenship is an alien element in the economic world outside. Social rights in their modern form imply an invasion of contract by status, the subordination of market price to social justice, the replacement of the free bargain by the declaration of rights. But are these principles quite foreign to the practice of the market to-day, or are they there already, entrenched within the contract system itself? I think it is clear that they are.

As I have already pointed out, one of the main achievements of political power in the nineteenth century was to clear the way for the growth of trade unionism by enabling the workers to use their civil rights collectively. This was an anomaly, because hitherto it was political rights that were used for collective action, through parliament and local councils, whereas civil rights were intensely individual, and had therefore harmonised with the individualism of early capitalism. Trade unionism created a sort of secondary industrial citizenship, which naturally became imbued with the spirit appropriate to an institution

68

of citizenship. Collective civil rights could be used, not merely for bargaining in the true sense of the term, but for the assertion of basic rights. The position was an impossible one and could only be transitional. Rights are not a proper matter for bargaining. To have to bargain for a living wage in a society which accepts the living wage as a social right is as absurd as to have to haggle for a vote in a society which accepts the vote as a political right. Yet the early twentieth century attempted to make sense of this absurdity. It fully endorsed collective bargaining as a normal and peaceful market operation, while recognising in principle the right of the citizen to a minimum standard of civilised living, which was precisely what the trade unions believed, and with good reason, that they were trying to win for their members with the weapon of the bargain.

In the outburst of big strikes immediately before the First World War this note of a concerted demand for social rights was clearly audible. The government was forced to intervene. It professed to do so entirely for the protection of the public, and pretended not to be concerned with the issues in dispute. In 1912 Mr Askwith, the chief negotiator, told Mr Asquith, the Prime Minister, that intervention had failed and government prestige had suffered. To which the Prime Minister replied: 'Every word you have spoken endorses the opinion I have formed. It is a degradation of government.'[1] History soon showed that such a view was a complete anachronism. The government can no longer stand aloof from industrial disputes,

[1] Lord Askwith, *Industrial Problems and Disputes*, p. 228.

as though the level of wages and the standard of living of the workers were matters with which it need not concern itself. And government intervention in industrial disputes has been met from the other side by trade union intervention in the work of government. This is both a significant and a welcome development, provided its implications are fully realised. In the past trade unionism had to assert social rights by attacks delivered from outside the system in which power resided. To-day it defends them from inside, in co-operation with government. On major issues crude economic bargaining is converted into something more like a joint discussion of policy.

The implication is that decisions reached in this way must command respect. If citizenship is invoked in the defence of rights, the corresponding duties of citizenship cannot be ignored. These do not require a man to sacrifice his individual liberty or to submit without question to every demand made by government. But they do require that his acts should be inspired by a lively sense of responsibility towards the welfare of the community. Trade union leaders in general accept this implication, but this is not true of all members of the rank and file. The traditions built up at a time when trade unions were fighting for their existence, and when conditions of employment depended wholly on the outcome of unequal bargaining, make its acceptance very difficult. Unofficial strikes have become very frequent, and it is clear that one important element in industrial disputes is discord between trade union leaders and certain sections of trade union members. Now duties can derive either from status or from contract.

Leaders of unofficial strikes are liable to reject both. The strikes usually involve breach of contract or the repudiation of agreements. Appeal is made to some allegedly higher principle—in reality, though this may not be expressly asserted, to the status rights of industrial citizenship. There are many precedents to-day for the subordination of contract to status. Perhaps the most familiar are to be found in our handling of the housing problem. Rents are controlled and the rights of occupants protected after their contracts have expired, houses are requisitioned, agreements freely entered into are set aside or modified by tribunals applying the principles of social equity and the just price. The sanctity of contract gives way to the requirements of public policy, and I am not suggesting for a moment that this ought not to be so. But if the obligations of contract are brushed aside by an appeal to the rights of citizenship, then the duties of citizenship must be accepted as well. In some recent unofficial strikes an attempt has, I think, been made to claim the rights both of status and of contract while repudiating the duties under both these heads.

But my main concern is, not with the nature of strikes, but rather with the current conception of what constitutes a fair wage. I think it is clear that this conception includes the notion of status. It enters into every discussion of wage rates and professional salaries. What *ought* a medical specialist or a dentist to earn, we ask? Would twice the salary of a university professor be about right, or is that not enough? And, of course, the system envisaged is one of stratified, not uniform, status. The claim is not merely for a basic living wage with such variations above that level as can be extracted by each grade from the conditions in the market at the moment. The claims of status are to a hierarchical wage structure, each level of which represents a social right and not merely a market value. Collective bargaining must involve, even in its elementary forms, the classification of workers into groups, or grades, within which minor occupational differences are ignored. As in mass schooling, so in mass employment, questions of rights, standards, opportunities and so forth can be intelligibly discussed and handled only in terms of a limited number of categories and by cutting up a continuous chain of differences into a series of classes whose names instantly ring the appropriate bell in the mind of the busy official. As the area of negotiation spreads, the assimilation of groups necessarily follows on the assimilation of individuals, until the stratification of the whole population of workers is, as far as possible, standardised. Only then can general principles of social justice be formulated. There must be uniformity within each grade, and difference between grades. These principles dominate the minds of those discussing wage claims, even though rationalisation produces other arguments, such as that profits are excessive and the industry can afford to pay higher wages, or that higher wages are necessary to maintain the supply of suitable labour or to prevent its decline.

The White Paper on Personal Incomes[1] flashed a beam of light into these dark places of the mind, but the end result has been only to make the process of rationalisation

[1] Cmd. 7321. 1948.

more intricate and laborious. The basic conflict between social rights and market value has not been resolved. One labour spokesman said: 'An equitable relationship must be established between industry and industry.'[1] An equitable relationship is a social, not an economic, concept. The General Council of the T.U.C. approved the principles of the White Paper to the extent that 'they recognise the need to safeguard those wage differentials which are essential elements in the wages structure of many important industries, and are required to sustain those standards of craftsmanship, training and experience that contribute directly to industrial efficiency and higher productivity'.[2] Here market value and economic incentive find a place in an argument which is fundamentally concerned with status. The White Paper itself took a rather different, and possibly a truer, view of differentials. 'The last hundred years have seen the growth of certain traditional or customary relationships between personal incomes—including wages and salaries—in different occupations.... These have no necessary relevance to modern conditions.' Tradition and custom are social, not economic, principles, and they are old names for the modern structure of status rights.

The White Paper stated frankly that differentials based on these social concepts could not satisfy current economic requirements. They did not provide the incentives needed

---

[1] As reported in *The Times*.

[2] Recommendations of the Special Committee on the Economic Situation as accepted by the General Council at their Special Meeting on 18 February 1948.

to secure the best distribution of labour. 'Relative income levels must be such as to encourage the movement of labour to those industries where it is most needed, and should not, as in some cases they still do, tempt it in a contrary direction.' Notice that it says '*still* do'. Once again the modern conception of social rights is treated as a survival from the dark past. As we go on, the confusion thickens. 'Each claim for an increase in wages or salaries must be considered on its national merits', that is, in terms of national policy. But this policy cannot be directly enforced by the exercise of the political rights of citizenship through government, because that would involve 'an incursion by the Government into what has hitherto been regarded as a field of free contract between individuals and organisations', that is, an invasion of the civil rights of the citizen. Civil rights are therefore to assume political responsibility, and free contract is to act as the instrument of national policy. And there is yet another paradox. The incentive that operates in the free contract system of the open market is the incentive of personal gain. The incentive that corresponds to social rights is that of public duty. To which is the appeal being made? The answer is, to both. The citizen is urged to respond to the call of duty by allowing some scope to the motive of individual self-interest. But these paradoxes are not the invention of muddled brains; they are inherent in our contemporary social system. And they need not cause us undue anxiety, for a little common sense can often move a mountain of paradox in the world of action, though logic may be unable to surmount it in the world of thought.

5. *Conclusions*

I have tried to show how citizenship, and other forces outside it, have been altering the pattern of social inequality. To complete the picture I ought now to survey the results as a whole on the structure of social class. They have undoubtedly been profound, and it may be that the inequalities permitted, and even moulded, by citizenship do not any longer constitute class distinctions in the sense in which that term is used of past societies. But to examine this question I should require another lecture, and it would probably consist of a mixture of dry statistics of uncertain meaning and meaningful judgements of doubtful validity. For our ignorance of this matter is profound. It is therefore perhaps fortunate for the reputation of sociology that I should be obliged to confine myself to a few tentative observations, made in an attempt to answer the four questions which I posed at the end of my introduction to my theme.

We have to look for the combined effects of three factors. First, the compression, at both ends, of the scale of income distribution. Second, the great extension of the area of common culture and common experience. And third, the enrichment of the universal status of citizenship, combined with the recognition and stabilisation of certain status differences chiefly through the linked systems of education and occupation. The first two have made the third possible. Status differences can receive the stamp of legitimacy in terms of democratic citizenship provided they do not cut too deep, but occur within a population united in a single civilisation; and provided they are not an expression of hereditary privilege. This means that inequalities can be tolerated within a fundamentally egalitarian society provided they are not dynamic, that is to say that they do not create incentives which spring from dissatisfaction and the feeling that 'this kind of life is not good enough for me', or 'I am determined that my son shall be spared what I had to put up with.' But the kind of inequality pleaded for in the White Paper can be justified only if it *is* dynamic, and if it *does* provide an incentive to change and betterment. It may prove, therefore, that the inequalities permitted, and even moulded, by citizenship will not function in an economic sense as forces influencing the free distribution of manpower. Or that social stratification persists, but social ambition ceases to be a normal phenomenon, and becomes a deviant behaviour pattern— to use some of the jargon of sociology.

Should things develop to such lengths, we might find that the only remaining drive with a consistent distributive effect—distributive, that is, of manpower through the hierarchy of economic levels—was the ambition of the schoolboy to do well in his lessons, to pass his examinations, and to win promotion up the educational ladder. And if the official aim of securing 'parity of esteem' between the three types of secondary school were realised, we might lose the greater part even of that. Such would be the extreme result of establishing social conditions in which every man was content with the station of life to which it had pleased citizenship to call him.

76

In saying this I have answered two of my four questions, the first and the last. I asked whether the sociological hypothesis latent in Marshall's essay is valid to-day, the hypothesis, namely, that there is a kind of basic human equality, associated with full community membership, which is not inconsistent with a superstructure of economic inequality. I asked, too, whether there was any limit to the present drive towards social equality inherent in the principles governing the movement. My answer is that the preservation of economic inequalities has been made more difficult by the enrichment of the status of citizenship. There is less room for them, and there is more and more likelihood of their being challenged. But we are certainly proceeding at present on the assumption that the hypothesis is valid. And this assumption provides the answer to the second question. We are not aiming at absolute equality. There are limits inherent in the egalitarian movement. But the movement is a double one. It operates partly through citizenship and partly through the economic system. In both cases the aim is to remove inequalities which cannot be regarded as legitimate, but the standard of legitimacy is different. In the former it is the standard of social justice, in the latter it is social justice combined with economic necessity. It is possible, therefore, that the inequalities permitted by the two halves of the movement will not coincide. Class distinctions may survive which have no appropriate economic function, and economic differences which do not correspond with accepted class distinctions.

My third question referred to the changing balance

77

between rights and duties. Rights have been multiplied, and they are precise. Each individual knows just what he is entitled to claim. The duty whose discharge is most obviously and immediately necessary for the fulfilment of the right is the duty to pay taxes and insurance contributions. Since these are compulsory, no act of will is involved, and no keen sentiment of loyalty. Education and military service are also compulsory. The other duties are vague, and are included in the general obligation to live the life of a good citizen, giving such service as one can to promote the welfare of the community. But the community is so large that the obligation appears remote and unreal. Of paramount importance is the duty to work, but the effect of one man's labour on the well-being of the whole society is so infinitely small that it is hard for him to believe that he can do much harm by withholding or curtailing it.

When social relations were dominated by contract, the duty to work was not recognised. It was a man's own affair whether he worked or not. If he chose to live idly in poverty, he was at liberty to do so, provided he did not become a nuisance. If he was able to live idly in comfort, he was regarded, not as a drone, but as an aristocrat—to be envied and admired. When the economy of this country was in process of transformation into a system of this kind, great anxiety was felt whether the necessary labour would be forthcoming. The driving forces of group custom and regulation had to be replaced by the incentive of personal gain, and grave doubts were expressed whether this incentive could be relied upon. This explains Colquhoun's views on poverty, and the pithy remark of Mandeville, that labourers 'have nothing to stir them up to be serviceable but their wants, which it is prudence to relieve but folly to cure'.[1] And in the eighteenth century their wants were very simple. They were governed by established class habits of living, and no continuous scale of rising standards of consumption existed to entice the labourers to earn more in order to spend more on desirable things hitherto just beyond their reach—like radio sets, bicycles, cinemas or holidays by the sea. The following comment by a writer in 1728, which is but one example from many in the same sense, may well have been based on sound observation. 'People in low life', he said, 'who work only for their daily bread, if they can get it by three days work in the week, will many of them make holiday the other three, or set their own price on their labour.'[2] And, if they adopted the latter course, it was generally assumed that they would spend the extra money on drink, the only easily available luxury. The general rise in the standard of living has caused this phenomenon, or something like it, to reappear in contemporary society, though cigarettes now play a more important role than drink.

It is no easy matter to revive the sense of the personal obligation to work in a new form in which it is attached to the status of citizenship. It is not made any easier by the fact that the essential duty is not to have a job and

[1] *The Fable of the Bees*, 6th ed. (1732), p. 213.
[2] E. S. Furniss, *The Position of the Laborer in a System of Nationalism*, p. 125.

79

hold it, since that is relatively simple in conditions of full employment, but to put one's heart into one's job and work hard. For the standard by which to measure hard work is immensely elastic. A successful appeal to the duties of citizenship can be made in times of emergency, but the Dunkirk spirit cannot be a permanent feature of any civilisation. Nevertheless, an attempt is being made by trade union leaders to inculcate a sense of this general duty. At a conference on 18 November of last year Mr Tanner referred to 'the imperative obligation on both sides of industry to make their full contribution to the rehabilitation of the national economy and world recovery'.[1] But the national community is too large and remote to command this kind of loyalty and to make of it a continual driving force. That is why many people think that the solution of our problem lies in the development of more limited loyalties, to the local community and especially to the working group. In this latter form industrial citizenship, devolving its obligations down to the basic units of production, might supply some of the vigour that citizenship in general appears to lack.

I come finally to the second of my original four questions, which was not, however, so much a question as a statement. I pointed out that Marshall stipulated that measures designed to raise the general level of civilisation of the workers must not interfere with the freedom of the market. If they did, they might become indistinguishable from socialism. And I said that obviously this limitation

---

[1] *The Times*, 19 November 1948.

on policy had since been abandoned. Socialist measures, in Marshall's sense, have been accepted by all political parties. This led me to the platitude that the conflict between egalitarian measures and the free market must be examined in the course of any attempt to carry Marshall's sociological hypothesis over into the modern age.

I have touched on this vast subject at several points, and in this concluding summary I will confine myself to one aspect of the problem. The unified civilisation which makes social inequalities acceptable, and threatens to make them economically functionless, is achieved by a progressive divorce between real and money incomes. This is, of course, explicit in the major social services, such as health and education, which give benefits in kind without any *ad hoc* payment. In scholarships and legal aid, prices scaled to money incomes keep real income relatively constant, in so far as it is affected by these particular needs. Rent restriction, combined with security of tenure, achieves a similar result by different means. So, in varying degrees, do rationing, food subsidies, utility goods and price controls. The advantages obtained by having a larger money income do not disappear, but they are confined to a limited area of consumption.

I spoke just now of the conventional hierarchy of the wage structure. Here importance is attached to differences in money income and the higher earnings are expected to yield real and substantial advantages—as, of course, they still do in spite of the trend towards the equalisation of real incomes. But the importance of wage differentials is, I am sure, partly symbolic. They operate as labels attached to industrial status, not only as instruments of genuine economic stratification. And we also see signs that the acceptance of this system of economic inequality by the workers themselves—especially those fairly low down in the scale—is sometimes counteracted by claims to greater equality with respect to those forms of real enjoyment which are not paid for out of wages. Manual workers may accept it as right and proper that they should earn less money than certain clerical grades, but at the same time wage-earners may press for the same general amenities as are enjoyed by salaried employees, because these should reflect the fundamental equality of all citizens and not the inequalities of earnings or occupational grades. If the manager can get a day off for a football match, why not the workman? Common enjoyment is a common right.

Recent studies of adult and child opinion have found that, when the question is posed in general terms, there is a declining interest in the earning of big money. This is not due, I think, only to the heavy burden of progressive taxation, but to an implicit belief that society should, and will, guarantee all the essentials of a decent and secure life at every level, irrespective of the amount of money earned. In a population of secondary schoolboys examined by the Bristol Institute of Education, 86% wanted an interesting job at a reasonable wage and only 9% a job in which they could make a lot of money. And the average intelligence quotient of the second group was 16 points lower than that of the first.[1] In a poll conducted by the British Insti-

[1] *Research Bulletin*, no. 11, p. 23.

tute of Public Opinion, 23% wanted as high wages as possible, and 73% preferred security at lower wages.[1] But at any given moment, and in response to a particular question about their present circumstances, most people, one would imagine, would confess to a desire for more money than they are actually getting. Another poll, taken in November 1947, suggests that even this expectation is exaggerated. For 51% said their earnings were at or above a level adequate to cover family needs, and only 45% that they were inadequate. The attitude is bound to vary at different social levels. The classes which have gained most from the social services, and in which real income in general has been rising, might be expected to be less preoccupied with differences in money income. But we should be prepared to find other reactions in that section of the middle classes in which the pattern of money incomes is at the moment most markedly incoherent, while the elements of civilised living traditionally most highly prized are becoming unattainable with the money incomes available—or by any other means.

The general point is one to which Professor Robbins referred when he lectured here two years ago. 'We are following', he said, 'a policy which is self-contradictory and self-frustrating. We are relaxing taxation and seeking, wherever possible, to introduce systems of payments which fluctuate with output. And, at the same time, our price fixing and the consequential rationing system are inspired by egalitarian principles. The result is that we

[1] January 1946.

get the worst of both worlds.'[1] And again: 'The belief that, in normal times, it is particularly sensible to try to mix the principles and run an egalitarian real income system side by side with an inegalitarian money income system seems to me somewhat *simpliste*.'[2] Yes, to the economist perhaps, if he tries to judge the situation according to the logic of a market economy. But not necessarily to the sociologist, who remembers that social behaviour is not governed by logic, and that a human society can make a square meal out of a stew of paradox without getting indigestion—at least for quite a long time. The policy, in fact, may not be *simpliste* at all, but subtle; a new-fangled application of the old maxim *divide et impera*—play one off against the other to keep the peace. But, more seriously, the word *simpliste* suggests that the antinomy is merely the result of the muddled thinking of our rulers and that, once they see the light, there is nothing to prevent them altering their line of action. I believe, on the contrary, that this conflict of principles springs from the very roots of our social order in the present phase of the development of democratic citizenship. Apparent inconsistencies are in fact a source of stability, achieved through a compromise which is not dictated by logic. This phase will not continue indefinitely. It may be that some of the conflicts within our social system are becoming too sharp for the compromise to achieve its purpose much longer. But, if we wish to assist in their resolution, we must try to understand their

[1] *The Economic Problem in Peace and War*, p. 9.
[2] *Ib.* p. 16.

84

deeper nature and to realise the profound and disturbing effects which would be produced by any hasty attempt to reverse present and recent trends. It has been my aim in these lectures to throw a little light on one element which I believe to be of fundamental importance, namely the impact of a rapidly developing concept of the rights of citizenship on the structure of social inequality.

(II)

SOCIAL CLASS—A PRELIMINARY
ANALYSIS[1]

1

I т is a bad thing for a subject when few people write on it
at length but many in brief. That is why the study of social
class is in so unhealthy a state. Every attempt at a general
systematic sociology must contain a chapter on it, and the
learned journals of Europe and America are sprinkled
with articles disputing its essential nature, arguing over
its definition or even denying its existence, yet recent
years have produced only one substantial work which
attempts a comprehensive view, that of Pontus Fahlbeck.[2]
Meanwhile studies have been made by historians and sociologists both of particular forms of class, such as slavery,
caste or the proletariat, and of the class structure of particular societies.[3] It can easily be argued that this is the
proper line of attack, and that these researches should be
allowed to progress further before any attempt at synthesis
or at general analysis is made. But there are two objections
to this view. In the first place, much labour may be wasted
if the researchers do not start with a fairly clear idea of the

[1] From *The Sociological Review*, vol. xxvi, no. 1, January 1934.
[2] P. Fahlbeck, *Die Klassen und die Gesellschaft*. There is also a short
study by G. Albrecht, *Die sozialen Klassen*. P. Sorokin's *Social Mobility*
rejects the concept of class in a general sense as unhelpful.
[3] A good example of the latter type of study is Th. Geiger, *Die
soziale Schichtung des deutschen Volkes*.

questions to which they are trying to find answers, and, unfortunately, the minor spate of literary fragments on the subject has succeeded in obscuring, rather than clarifying, the issue. In the second place, there is a grave danger of treating class in isolation from other social institutions, or even of treating a particular form of class apart from the class structure of the society as a whole. Some writers, studying social evolution, describe the addition of class to class in a manner which implies that the arrival of the new left the character and personality of the old unchanged.[1] The class theory of Marx is based on a thoroughly comprehensive view of the social process, but this did not prevent Engels from tracing the life-history of the bourgeoisie from the feudal to the capitalist age, during which time it changed its personnel, its whole character, and its place in the social hierarchy, but, apparently, succeeded in preserving its identification disc intact for the benefit of future historians.[2]

This is my justification for attempting yet another analysis of the concept, social class. But, at the very outset, we meet a serious difficulty. If we start with a word—class—we have already made important assumptions. We are assuming that, because the word is commonly and usefully employed, it must express a definable concept. We may proceed to review all the objects which it generally denotes and to identify the concept by ob-

[1] Cf. Th. Geiger, 'Zur Theorie des Klassenbegriffs', in Schmoller's *Jahrbuch*, vol. 54, p. 390, where he criticises Vierkandt for falling into this error. Also L. Gumplowicz, *Grundriss der Soziologie*, ch. 3, § 2.
[2] *Socialism, Utopian and Scientific.* Introduction.

SOCIAL CLASS—A PRELIMINARY ANALYSIS

serving their common characteristics. We may then exercise our ingenuity in composing a definition that covers all known varieties, and, in fact, behave exactly like an International Conference achieving unanimity through a formula. This process, when thus crudely described, appears obviously futile. But it is not easy to shake oneself entirely free from the tyranny of words. We can trace it in the work of Robert Michels, who spends much time in a vain search for a satisfactory criterion, and rejects them all,[1] and also in that of Paul Mombert, who insists on a comprehensive definition and consequently stresses unimportant similarities at the expense of important differences.[2] A definition of this kind has little heuristic value, since it excludes nothing that is comparable with what it includes. The alternative is to start at the other end, the factual end, using the word 'class' merely as a finger-post indicating the general direction of our researches, and to classify the relevant observed phenomena on the basis of the similarities and differences which are significant for social analysis, without caring whether the resulting concepts are or are not possessed of names. If names do not exist, we can invent them. If this is our method, we can legitimately begin with the study of any one society that seems suitable, and we shall not thereby become guilty of the sin of which Mombert accuses Sombart, that of defining the general concept 'class' by means of evidence taken

---

[1] 'Beitrag zur Lehre von der Klassenbildung', *Archiv für Sozialwissenschaft*, vol. XLIX.
[2] 'Zum Wesen der sozialen Klasse', in *Hauptprobleme der Soziologie*, especially p. 244.

from one instance only. The universality of the phenomena described remains an open question until tested by
comparison. Nevertheless, the analysis of the particular
example may yield results capable of general application,
provided it is interpreted, not merely in terms of external
form, but with reference to fundamental social functions
and social relations.

Let us take, then, as our finger-post, not merely 'class',
but 'social class', and as our instance, contemporary
England. The investigator who chooses his own society
as his field of research is able to use the knowledge he can
derive from intuition and observation as a guide in his
analysis. Social class is a phenomenon of which he has
direct personal experience as a force in his own life. He
can say, with certainty, what it is not. He can frame
a working hypothesis of what it is. That is the purpose of
this article. It may not be necessary to mention contemporary England again, but the whole analysis will be
made in the light of my knowledge of the society in which
I live. My object is to describe a fact, not to define a word,
but to describe it by resolving it into simple concepts,
into fundamental social principles, which can serve as
tools for wider research operations. When I speak of
social class in this article, it is to be understood in this
restricted sense.

2

It is important to realize what a large variety of groups
must be excluded before we arrive at even the broadest
conception of class. It is not merely that we exclude

natural or statistical groups which have no social significance, and also kinship groups, local communities,
and religious and political organisations.[1] We do not
include such highly significant classes as married women,
lunatics, old age pensioners, and motorists. Yet it is not
easy to explain why they should be left out if occupational
groups are to be put into the list merely because they are
conspicuous social aggregations. Othmar Spann con-
spicuously fails to answer this question, and his article
on *Klasse und Stand*[2] is really an article on such social
groups as happen to have taken his fancy. The method of
cataloguing the various foundations on which such groups
may be built—as property, occupation, political power,
etc.—is bound to be illustrative rather than exhaustive,
and there remains a vague and undefined residue which
contains precisely that form of grouping which, led by
the finger-post 'social class', we are looking for in contemporary England.

What, then, are the qualities which we know to belong
to this phenomenon that we wish to describe and analyse?
First, it represents a hierarchical social stratification. It is
concerned with vertical, not horizontal, social distance.
Occupational groups—the German *Berufsstände*—which
may stand two or three or many on a level, must be excluded. They are of great social importance and they may
play a part in the formation of social class, but in themselves they are something different. Secondly, the hier-

[1] Cf. Schmoller's definition, which begins with a list of excluded
groups. *Die soziale Frage*, p. 142.
[2] *Handwörterbuch der Staatswissenschaft.*

archy, the relationship of inferiority and superiority, is not based merely on natural differences. It requires social recognition. The natural superiority of the leader over the follower is not of the nature of social class. The respect of the lower for the higher is direct and spontaneous (though related to social function), not induced and conventional. Thirdly, there is some permanence in the grouping, so that a man who belongs to a certain class remains in it unless—to use a colloquialism—'something is done about it', in contrast to age-groups, between which mobility is automatic.

The implications of these last two points need to be further examined. Point three does not follow logically from point two; it is a separate observation. Society could—and some societies do—recognise age as the basis of a hierarchy. But in our society social class is conceived as having stability. This is essential to it, and differentiates it radically from a system of seniority. We must, therefore, ask what, exactly, social recognition means. Is it merely a formal acknowledgment of a pre-existent fact, like the hall-mark on gold, or the bestowal at will of a new character, like the stamp on the guinea? And, if it is the former, are these facts, these insignia of social class, attributes which an individual has normally a reasonable chance of acquiring by his own effort? It is clear that society is not even as free to bestow class status as a monarch is to bestow rank and titles, although the monarch is by custom expected to pay heed to the pre-existent fact of merit. The vast majority of individuals class themselves by virtue of the possession of certain attributes. But even so, recognition is not merely a hall-mark. Society does

not recognise a bourgeois in the sense in which an ento-
mologist recognises a beetle or a violin expert a Stradi-
varius. Recognition implies the admission to certain
social relationships, and therefore, to use Max Weber's
peculiar term, the offer of a certain *Lebenschance*.[1] We
must not interpret this, as he does, in a purely economic
sense as describing the individual's position in relation to
the market. It is equally applicable to social opportunity.
Social class, as distinct from technical or financial endow-
ments, can influence a man's economic *Lebenschance*. It
may affect his selection for certain kinds of employment.
A landlord may reject a perfectly solvent tenant as un-
desirable on the grounds of his class, which he regards as
an index of his probable behaviour. But it is also far more
generally operative in determining the possibilities of
social intercourse that lie open to him, marriage, social
mixing and the admission to associations of all kinds.
I submit, therefore, that, if we are thinking of a social class
as a group based on a certain resemblance of its members,
we must regard it as a group of persons with similar social
chances, rather than as a group of persons with similar
internal or external attributes. The essence of social class
is the way a man is treated by his fellows (and, reciprocally,
the way he treats them), not the qualities or the possessions
which cause that treatment. It would be possible, and perhaps useful, to group people simply in terms of their attributes, without asking how those attributes affected their
social relations, but the result would be a study of social
types, not of social classes.

[1] *Wirtschaft und Gesellschaft*, pt. III, ch. 4.

Social recognition is, therefore, an important factor even though, in the great majority of cases, a man's social class is indubitably determined by the circumstances of his life. These may be divided into the experience, environment, and education which have moulded his character and habits during childhood and youth, on the one hand, and the external assets and the skill and knowledge which he may acquire later in life by his own deliberate effort, on the other hand. It is on the former, relatively unalterable, qualities that social class is conceived to be based, but the latter have their share of influence. They may claim, though not command, recognition. Wealth, for example, sometimes secures direct admission into the upper ranks of society on its own account. More often it is allowed to count as a compensation for deficiencies in the intrinsic personal qualities normally belonging to the members of the class. But the main service of wealth is to purchase the environment which, given time enough, will produce the intrinsic qualities. This fact further increases the importance of social recognition, which can determine how much weight is to be given to those insignia of class which can be most easily obtained or most plausibly imitated.

This view implies the rejection of the purely objective theories which represent class as automatically determined by definite criteria, especially wealth and occupation, and also the purely subjective theories according to which a man belongs to the class that he feels he belongs to, whose class-consciousness he shares.[1] The adherents of the latter theory are inclined to say that a man can enter a class by

[1] For a classification of theories on this basis, see Mombert, *op. cit.*

adopting the views that are characteristic of it and by becoming a supporter of its interests. They would agree, therefore, with Ferdinand Tönnies that the ideal type of the class is the party,[1] and with Theodor Geiger that the proletariat includes sympathetic socialist intellectuals.[2] I have suggested that the objectivity of class consists, not in the criteria that distinguish it, but in the social relations that it produces, and its subjectivity in the basic need for mutual conscious recognition.

3

The next proposition is, again, not an inference from any premise, but the fruit of observation. There are many principles on which a society may be divided into groups. There are several on which it may be stratified into layers. But social class is a single principle which can only produce one result. It permeates the whole community, so that its application yields a single scheme of location which, in theory, assigns a place to every component part of the whole. It may appear as though clearly defined class groups exist only at the top and bottom of society, and not in the middle. But we know that social class enters into the life of every member of the community, because our society is possessed of a class system. It recognises this form of differentiation as a force affecting social behaviour and social opportunity. It is true that this proposition, especially when applied to other societies than our own, produces untidy results, but that is not a sufficient reason for

[1] 'Stände und Klassen', in *Handwörterbuch der Soziologie*.
[2] 'Zur Theorie des Klassenbegriffs', pp. 421 *et seq.*

abandoning it. It is difficult, for instance, to say that the classes of peasant-proprietor and urban bourgeois can be fitted into a single social scale, one above the other, although it is clear that they belong to the same principle of classification. The answer is that they are the results of applying the same principle to different communities. There is a federal character in organised society: within the major community minor communities exist. The more heterogeneous the major community, the more unlikely it is to have a simple class structure. In such a case we may say that there is a national class system, in the sense, only, that class is a feature of the lives of all nationals, but that there are no national classes. To add to the confusion, it is quite possible that there may be *one* national class, an aristocracy, the only group that has achieved national unity, but it will be the product of a class system that permeates the whole. There is nothing disturbing in this thought, and we must not try to impose on our subject a clarity and symmetry which it does not by nature possess.

Other important conclusions follow from this conception of social class as a stratification of a community. We may recall the sense in which Professor McIver uses this term. 'The mark of a community', he writes, 'is that one's life *may* be lived wholly within it, that all one's social relations *may* be found within it.'[1] This rightly emphasises the fact that a community is concerned with human activities regarded not merely as means, but as the ends of life. It is obvious that the same activity frequently, or even normally, figures in both categories, but the two

[1] *Society, its Structure and Changes*, p. 10.

aspects lead to different mental orientations and to different social patterns. Many cultural associations exist for the pursuit of special ends, but a community pursues them all. Social class, as a section of a community, retains this essential character. One or two illustrations will make this point clear. In all societies social class is concerned with the selection of occupations, that is, with economic means, but the connexion is derived from a conventional view of the proper way for a man of given station to 'occupy himself'. The occupation is here being considered as an end, as a part of the whole pattern of human living. If we look back to the time when gentlemen were not supposed to engage in trade, we can see that this was not because trade was an inadequate means for procuring the income required to support a gentleman's life, but because trade itself was thought incompatible with the ideal of what a gentleman's life should be.

If social class is concerned with *all* ends, it follows that it must be bi-sexual, since a complete community life of men or women only is inconceivable. Observation confirms this inference. A group of men endowed with rank or titles for which only men are eligible may play an important part in the formation of classes, but it is not a social class. For our purposes the significant group created by the English peerage is not composed of the men who sit in the House of Lords, but includes their families and relatives of both sexes through several degrees of affinity. The 'professional class' is not co-terminous with the members of the professions. Wherever women take their social position from their fathers and husbands, social class is effectively determined by the status of men, but it is not composed of men. We cannot accept the familiar generalisation that class tends to endogamy and also speak, in a literal sense, of a military class, since there are obvious difficulties in the way of making an army endogamous.

This can be expressed by saying that the true unit of social class is the family. This has been said by Joseph Schumpeter, but he does not build on the statement and seems later actually to abandon it.[1] He appears to be thinking of the important fact that, however mobile the society, every child is classed at birth by the circumstances of its birth. This confirms the rejection both of the purely subjective view of class and of the objective view which relates it directly to the intrinsic qualities of the individual. The new-born infant is not class-conscious and is, socially speaking, intrinsically nothing, and yet there is no doubt that it belongs to a class and that this fact determines its *Lebenschance*. But it is more important, because less easy, to remember that social class reproduces the quality of the family as a form of association for the satisfaction of non-specialised social ends.

4

It is sometimes said that the force which unites a social class is 'consciousness of kind'. Giddings used this phrase with a precise, but quite different, meaning.[2] If we abandon his interpretation, the whole emphasis is thrown on

[1] 'Die sozialen Klassen im ethnisch homogenen Milieu', in *Archiv für Soʒialwissenschaft*, vol. LVII, p. 12. But cf. p. 29.
[2] *Principles of Sociology*, pp. 17 and 124–31.

the word 'kind', and we are offering a synonym, not a definition. 'Kind' is simply that particular sort of similarity which builds social classes and not trade unions, literary societies, political parties or county associations. We must try to do better than this.

Social ties may be classified as being based either on difference or on similarity. Difference unites by creating the possibility of reciprocal service. Similarity unites most obviously through the recognition of a common interest, and less obviously as representing the easiest antithesis to isolation. Difference most readily suggests pairs, such as husband and wife, doctor and patient, master and pupil. Similarity suggests groups, such as nationalities, occupational associations or primitive age groups. The reciprocal pair may be enlarged by introducing other co-operating differences, as by adding the child to husband and wife or the nurse to doctor and patient. If we merely multiply both sides of a reciprocal pair, we get two reciprocal groups of similars, or identity groups, as we may briefly term them, as when master and pupil are enlarged to become staff and students. The existence of a reciprocal pair usually implies a basic element of identity. Marriage is a union of different sexes, but is normally built on similarities of race and culture. The reciprocal pair takes shape within a wider identity group. And yet, how slender this basis may be is seen if we consider how closely the relation of doctor to patient resembles that of horse-leech to horse.

This brings out the two functions of the identity group. It may be the necessary background for the formation of reciprocal ties, or it may be one half of a multiple reciprocal pair. If we consider, for example, a typical London club, it is clear that the members are united by their identity of sex, class and general culture, and yet, if they were identical in all respects, it would be a very dull affair. The purpose of the club is not simply to satisfy a desire to move among reproductions of oneself (though such a desire exists), but to exploit those minor personal differences of character, taste, and opinions which are found within the otherwise homogeneous milieu. The club is thus self-contained so far as its purpose is concerned, and is not organised with a view to co-operation or competition with bodies outside itself. The trade union, on the other hand, though it utilizes differences of ability in its members for organisation and leadership, is, as an organ of collective bargaining, a body in which members become as undifferentiated as the units in a mathematical calculation and the whole energy of the group is focused on its own reciprocal relationship with another group outside.

Now clearly any sense of similarity within a group implies a consciousness of difference from those not of the group. This is, in the case of the club, a matter of comparison, but, in the case of the trade union, a matter of relational contacts. Of these two types of group, the identity group utilizing subsidiary differences for mutual advantage and conscious of its identity through comparison with those outside, and the identity group organised for reciprocal relational contacts with one or more other groups, social class belongs to the former. It does, however, frequently develop the characteristics of the latter in addition. But a group of type two, which lacks the characteristics of type one, is not a social class. A working class, which is a real sphere of social intercourse of all kinds, may become so conscious of its antagonism to capital as to qualify for inclusion under type two. But it remains a social class. A working-class organization, possibly composed of men only, which is occupied entirely with the defence of its interests against capital, belongs rather to the category of party. This distinction might be translated into the terms used by McIver and others by saying that social class is based rather on similarity of attitudes than on identity of interests.

It follows from everything that has been said so far that social class is a derivative of the whole social personality of the individual, not of a mere facet of it, such as some technical equipment and the interests it may create. Social class is a human aggregation which has not been submitted to that splitting of individuality into its associative elements so subtly analysed by Simmel.[1] Each member mirrors in the microcosm of his personality the many-featured image of his class. Loyalty to class is, in a peculiar sense, loyalty to self. Class-consciousness is akin to consciousness of nationality, and nationality is not a specialism, not, like a profession or an income or a belief, detachable in thought from the whole personality. And yet class is alterable. Movement within one generation is not impossible: movement within two is common. Class-consciousness may, therefore, be combined with an ambition to rise, or to enable one's children to rise. This has led to the assertion that *dis*loyalty is a characteristic

[1] *Soziologie,* ch. 6.

feature of social classes.[1] This is a misleading generalisation. The distinctive characteristic is rather the markedly egoistic quality of class-consciousness. An individual's behaviour is conditioned by his class, but he does not . behave as a representative of it and he does not betray it by aspiring to leave it.

This word 'representative' may lead to confusion, since it has two meanings. We say a man is 'representative of his group' when we mean he is typical of it. But when we say he is 'a representative of his group', we mean that he is fulfilling a function with regard to it which involves a submission of his individuality to a cause. In the former case he is merely himself, but it is a self that can easily be matched. In the second case he is something besides himself, and also something less than himself. When two foreigners meet in peaceful conversation, their attitudes are greatly affected by their different nationalities, and this is a difference of which they are both conscious. And yet the relationship is entirely personal, the nationality expressing itself through the individual it has created. They meet as the products, not as the representatives, of their environing social groups. But when two enemy foreigners meet in time of war, each sees within and behind | the man who confronts him the image of the group which he represents. It is a meeting of two conflicting interests, two fragments of personalities, two points on the perimeters of two vastly greater wholes. Social classes may also be at war, in thought or in deed, and the same result

[1] W. Sulzbach, 'Die "Klasse" und der Klassenkampf', in *Archiv für Sozialwissenschaft*, vol. LXIII, pp. 305–6.

ensues. But the foundation of social class, discernible beneath such conscious antagonism and often existing without it, is the fact of 'representativeness' in the wider, less specialised sense.

5

Many writers try to elucidate the nature of classes by assigning certain attributes to each. The middle classes are puritanical, the capitalists are acquisitive, the peasants are conservative, and so forth.[1] Such phrases do not give us a definition. They do not mean that, in a strict logical sense, middle class connotes Puritanism and peasantry conservatism. There is no intention of maintaining that, if a man is not conservative, he cannot be a peasant. All that this process amounts to is a vague indication of the characteristics one may expect to find widely present within a group, the existence and general boundaries of which have been assumed as determined by other criteria. Those who correlate each class, not with abstract qualities, but with external facts like income or occupation, generally use these concepts in the same vague way. When they are used with precision—as they can be—as the connotations of the class name, the result is the identification of groups which may be of great social importance, but which are not identical with the phenomenon of social class as understood in this paper.[2]

[1] E.g. Arthur Bauer, *Les classes sociales*, which is a very naïve example of this method.

[2] This is clearly recognised by Mombert in his article, 'Die Tatsachen der Klassenbildung', in Schmoller's *Jahrbuch*, vol. XLIV, in which he attempts a statistical study of mobility.

Now, if such phrases as 'peasants are conservative' and 'Englishmen love games' do not indicate connotations, what do they mean? They may be a loose way of saying that these are attributes of a majority of the group. But to say that 'Englishmen love games' because a majority are sportsmen is only one degree less foolish than to say 'Englishmen are women' because a majority of the population is female. Sociology is not interested in proportions, but in relationships and the behaviour that results from them. But the words may be intended to suggest a different idea; they may mean that the love of games is sufficiently prevalent in England to leave its mark on the customary and institutional behaviour of the society. It affects not only the game-lovers but also the unsporting. It is part of a social environment with which they all come into contact. In this case we are not making a qualitative judgement of every individual and then a quantitative assessment of the results, but we are making a single qualitative judgement of the society. It is a judgement which can be tested and given precision by a more detailed examination of the ways in which this partiality for sport affects the general pattern of social behaviour. In this way our attention is diverted from the concept of a group of persons who resemble one another in their love of games to the concept of the pursuit of games as a force operating throughout the society. The group may be a reality, but it is not the whole reality, and its frontiers are indeterminate.

An illustration nearer to our theme can be found in the social significance of age. In some societies age is made the basis of a hierarchy of groups with social functions and specific relations to one another, which influence the behaviour of the individual members. In our society there is no such system of groups, and yet age is a fact to which some social meaning is attached, so that it affects social precedence, rights to property, claims to promotion, and many other things. At every level there is a large, but indeterminate, number of persons who are conscious of their resemblance in this respect and are thereby drawn together—or would be, if they met—into something in the nature of an age-group. But such groups are only incidental. At certain selected levels much sharper lines are drawn, creating such groups as infants, adults, and pensioners. But such groups tell only a part of the story. The same principle, age, which creates them also operates *within* them to produce subtler stratifications. So it is with social class. There is a customary standard of superiority and inferiority which operates throughout the community, contributing to determine for every individual his relations with other individuals and his access to social and economic opportunity. At every level there is a number of persons who recognise—or would, if they met—their objective similarities. These may be regarded as constituting a group, but it is easy to exaggerate the importance of such a concept. In the first place, the membership is fluctuating and indeterminate, and it is doubtful whether it can even theoretically be ascertained. In the second place, since social class implies a consciousness of a position with reference to other persons, a consciousness of social distance, no group is really helpful for its elucidation unless it is composed of persons in whom this consciousness takes the form of the recognition of membership of the group. Such a group would have a quasi-associational character which is not necessarily present in a social class. To return to the analogy, I know that there are others of the same age as myself, who might be regarded as a group, and I recognise them when we meet and my behaviour is affected by the fact, but my consciousness of age as a factor in social behaviour does not take the form of a feeling of group-membership. It is a personal consciousness which guides my behaviour in each situation, in each relationship, as it arises. The existence of the group is inferred, rather than felt. Undoubtedly any consciousness of class has more sense of the group in it than this, but this sense is probably strongest with regard to the division of society into three or four main strata, the upper class, the upper middle, lower middle, and lower classes. And the identification of these as groups cannot tell the whole story, since the same principle of class which creates them also operates within them to produce subtler differentiations.

To sum up: it may be impossible in our society to discover any definable groups which can be called social classes and which do not intermingle and overlap. It does not follow that class is a declining or an insignificant factor in our social life. The selection of the most obvious objective criteria may show us only potential, and not actual, social groups. It does not follow that class is only a potential force. Professor Sorokin dismisses class as a sociologists' myth.[1] Others declare that only one true class exists to-day, the proletariat. Von Wiese calls to his aid his curious concept of the 'abstract crowd' (*die abstrakte Masse*), a group that is not yet a group but which contains potentialities of common action.[2] I prefer to stress the institutional character of class as against the associational character of classes and to think in terms of a force rather than of groups. It is institutional in the sense that it is a social principle which presses individual behaviour into socially-determined moulds and produces uniformities of conduct in those who conform to custom. This view may involve only a difference of emphasis, but it has the value of guarding us against an underestimate of the importance of this force of class in a society which possesses no definable classes and of preventing much useless labour and

---

[1] *Note added in* 1949: In his recent book *Society, Culture and Personality* (p. 293, note) Professor Sorokin says that my interpretation of his position 'as denying the existence of social classes is grossly inaccurate'. He contends that social class is 'one of the multibonded groups and stratifications'. I admit that my curt reference to his theory is inadequate, and offer my belated apologies for what I wrote fifteen years ago. I was relying on the general treatment of the subject in *Social Mobility* and in particular on the passage on p. 18 which begins: 'This is the reason why I do not use the term "social classes" in a general sense and prefer to talk separately of the economic, the occupational and the political strata or classes.' Professor Sorokin then dismisses a whole series of definitions of the term 'social class' in a general sense as unhelpful and confusing, and reasserts his preference for studying the three kinds of stratification separately.

[2] Sorokin, *Social Mobility*, p. 18; Sulzbach, *loc. cit.* p. 299; L. D. Pesl, 'Mittelstandsfragen', in *Grundriss der Sozialökonomik*, pt. IX, vol. I; Carr Saunders and Caradog Jones, *Social Structure of England and Wales*, ch. 6; von Wiese, *System der allgemeinen Soziologie*, pt. III, ch. 2 and 6.

many futile squabbles on the part of those who persist in the attempt to find the true insignia of these social groups.[1]

6

It remains to examine very briefly the relation between the concept of social class outlined here and the class theory of Karl Marx. For Marx class is the principal dynamic force in the process of social change. It arises from the relations which are inherent in the productive system. These relations vary through time and are also numerous in any one period. Marx recognised several classes in nineteenth-century Europe, in particular the landowners, the greater bourgeoisie, the lesser bourgeoisie, the proletariat, and the slum proletariat.[2] Progress, according to the Marxian dialectic, is revolutionary. Each system moves towards a qualitative perfection and at the same time produces its own negation which brings about an abrupt qualitative change into something new and different. In its perfect state it is dominated by one relationship,[3] that between the ruling class, which impresses its

[1] G. L. Duprat, 'Soziale Typen oder soziale Klassen?', in *Jahrbuch für Soziologie*, vol. I, puts forward a theory somewhat similar to this, but he is more uncompromising in his denial of the existence of classes as groups.

[2] *Capital*, vol. III, ch. 52, gives three classes. There are longer lists in *The Communist Manifesto*, and in *The Eighteenth Brumaire of Louis Bonaparte* (trans. E. and C. Paul), pp. 32 and 44.

[3] 'Under all forms of society there is a certain industry which predominates over all the rest and whose condition therefore determines the rank and influence of all the rest. It is the universal light with which all the other colours are tinged and are modified through its peculiarity.' *Contribution to the Critique of Political Economy* (trans. N. I. Stone), p. 302. Compare the very similar approach of Sombart. A class 'is

ideology on the whole society, and the subject class which it requires as an instrument to its ends, but which will ultimately overthrow it. These alone are the 'revolutionary' classes.[1] This is the nature of that clear-cut social dichotomy towards which capitalist society was asserted to be advancing. When the revolutionary crisis occurs, it springs from the conscious antagonism of two groups of a quasi-associational character.

Now it is clear that the essential factor in this theory is the conception of these production-relations as forces determining the life-situation of individuals. Since many people are involved in similar relationships, they produce recognisable groups, but these are at first only of a statistical nature. Capital creates a mass of people in a common situation, and 'this mass is already a class, as opposed to capital, but not yet for itself'. In the struggle the mass unites 'to form a class and therewith to form a party',[2] but it only acquires this reality as a group when it has ceased to correspond to the relationship which created it. The proletariat is distinguished by an attitude, a policy, an ideology, which may be rejected by some wage-earners and adopted by some members of the bourgeoisie.[3] The final social dichotomy does not imply that

a social group, the individuals of which are the representatives of some economic system'. *Socialism and the Social Movement*, pp.1–2.

[1] *The Communist Manifesto* (ed. Ryazanoff), p. 26; cf. Marx's severe criticism of the Gotha Programme for its failure to realize the revolutionary character of the bourgeoisie.

[2] *The Poverty of Philosophy* (trans. Quelch), p. 158; *Communist Manifesto*, p. 37.

[3] Cf. *Communist Manifesto*, p. 38.

everyone is either a capitalist or a wage-earner, but that the relation between these two functional groups has so decisive an influence on the economic life of the whole society that everyone, even though not directly involved, is compelled to take up an attitude with regard to it and to assimilate himself to a class to which, by objective criteria, he does not belong.[1] It is not surprising, therefore, that when at last Marx attempted to define his classes and enumerate their insignia, he began hopelessly to flounder. The chapter in which Engels incorporated his notes was never finished, but there is enough to show that he was heading for disaster and that he was not perturbed. It mattered little that he could not define his groups or even prove their existence: he had no doubt at all about the reality of his social forces. Even in England the stratification was not found in its pure form, 'however, this is immaterial for our analysis'.[2]

In this respect, then, there is a resemblance between the method of Marx and the method I have attempted to follow above, but the subject-matter differs. It is not enough to say that Marx's classes are economic and mine social, his concerned with production and mine mainly with consumption, his with activities regarded as means

[1] Cf. John R. Commons, 'Is Class Conflict in America growing and is it Inevitable?', in *American Journal of Sociology*, vol. XIII, p. 756. He estimates that more than two-thirds of the occupied males in the U.S.A. are 'spectators' in the class struggle, but the importance of the conflict cannot be measured by the numbers involved.

[2] *Capital*, vol. III, ch. 52; cf. Cooley's judgement of classes in America. 'A conflict of class interests is, in great degree, not a conflict of persons but rather one of ideas in a common social medium.' *Social Organisation*, p. 242.

and mine with activities regarded as ends, though all these judgements contain some element of truth. Nor would the distinction between them be rendered unimportant if we were to agree with what Marx would undoubtedly maintain, that my classes are a mere insignificant by-product of his. They would not thereby become unworthy of analysis. And, in fact, there is a very important qualitative difference between them. Adopting the terminology suggested above, we can say that my social classes are identity groups existing for the sake of the internal contacts which the identity makes possible. Marx's classes are identity groups representing the two members of a reciprocal pair and using the identity as a means for influencing the relationship that makes the pair. His classes are marked by the overwhelming importance of external contacts which are, in fact, the sole cause of their existence. Mine are marked by the relative absence of such contacts and the relative self-sufficiency of the group for its own purposes. The borderline between my classes is defined by an attitude of comparison which recognises qualitative differences. The borderline between his classes is defined in terms of functional interaction.

It is tempting to seek analogies between this distinction and that between the German concepts of *Stand* and *Klasse*, usually translated as 'estate' and 'class'. Werner Sombart speaks of estates as organically related, classes as mechanically related. The estate regards itself as a member of a greater whole whose interests it serves. A class is, with regard to the whole society, self-seeking, disruptive, annihilating, pursuing its own interests with-

out respect to other groups.[1] Others put it that estates
co-operate and classes conflict, and that when an estate
manifests open social antagonism, it becomes a class.
Slavery is an estate until the slaves rebel.[2] Such a classification appears to me invalid, and it obscures the really
significant differences between the types of group viewed
in this particular aspect of their functional relationship.
Three concepts can be distinguished. There is first the
functional group which is self-sufficient for the performance of its own function and is placed thereby in a definite
relationship, not with any one other group, but with the
whole community. They are exemplified in the old German jingle, *Lehr-*, *Wehr-* and *Nährstände*, in many
legends, such as those found in Scandinavia and Persia,
which represent these groups as natural creations with
physical differences,[3] and find a close parallel in modern
society in the professions, though these have a more
definitely associational character. Together they make up
a pattern of social co-operation, and the question whether
the terms of co-operation are acceptable to all members
is a secondary one. Secondly, there are the functional
groups which exist only by virtue of their functional
interaction with another group. It is through this rela-

---

[1] *Moderne Kapitalismus*, vol. II, pt. 2, pp. 1091–3.

[2] Tönnies, *loc. cit.* K. Bauer-Mengelberg, 'Stand und Klasse', in
Kölner Vierteljahrshefte für Soziologie, vol. III. The latter maintains that
an Estate War is possible if the conflict is not over the place of each
combatant in the social organism, but over the nature of the social
organism itself.

[3] Cf. Sombart, *Moderne Kapitalismus*, vol. II, pt. 2, p. 1092. 'Sie
verdanken ihre Entstehung einem natürlichen Schöpfungsvorgang.'

tionship that their productive function is performed. Each relationship creates a pair, and no pair is collectively equal to the whole community. These are classes in the Marxian sense, and I would include, not only capital and labour, landlord and tenant, but also, in spite of the assertion of Mises[1] that this is not a production relationship, lord and serf. One group may combine both characters, as was clearly the case in the medieval conception of a servile class. It is probable that an analysis of attitudes during the General Strike would reveal a similar combination of ideas. The relation of capital to labour is of such universal importance that it easily became confused with the relation of labour as a functional estate to the community as a whole. The strikers, therefore, found it difficult to believe that anyone could honestly hold that the community existed as a third party. Finally, there are the social classes which I have been discussing which are not based on functional relationships at all. Anyone who reads Sombart's little essay, *Das Proletariat*, can see at once that he is there concerned with this third aspect of the class, and not with the functional aspect which is the main theme of his larger works. The investigation of this aspect also reveals further stratifications within the wage-earning class, which, under the Marxian analysis, appears as a homogeneous unit. In the case of the bourgeoisie it not only reveals a similar subdivision, but also suggests that what unity the bourgeoisie possesses as a social class is not derived directly from the relation of capital to labour. Capitalists, in the sense of owners of property, do show

[1] *Die Gemeinwirtschaft*, pp. 322–4.

common features when examined in terms of social class, but these are not derived from the fact that capital gives power over labour, nor primarily from the fact that capital yields an income, but rather from the fact that property, however small, gives security and insurance against misfortune and liberty for new adventure, thus cultivating a sense of proprietorship in a civilisation, of independence of status, which makes governments appear as servants, not as masters, and institutions as the means to freedom, not to servitude.

I offer these considerations as suggestions for a preliminary hypothesis, in the hope that they may help to guide and clarify the work of detailed research, and in particular in order to combat the ideas that because classes are hard to identify class is non-existent, and that, because the possible bases of classification are numerous, therefore they are infinite and lead into a morass from which no traveller can hope to extricate himself.

(III)

THE NATURE OF CLASS CONFLICT[1]

IF the subject of this Conference means anything at all, we must assume that an interpretation is being given to the word 'class' which implies that all group conflicts are not class conflicts. We are discussing a particular kind of group, whose nature is indicated by the phrase 'social stratification'. The groups, that is to say, lie one above the other in layers. It is the business of this Conference to discover whether such groups exist and, if so, how they behave. It is my special task to distinguish and classify the different forms of conflict that occur between them. Conflict between two firms or two nations does not enter into the classification, although it may play a part as evidence helping us to understand—or perhaps to dismiss as an illusion—conflict between social strata.

We think of 'a class' as a group of people. But we can also think of 'class' as a force or mechanism that operates to produce certain social attitudes. I like to begin my definition of class in this second sense by saying that it is a force that unites into groups people who differ from one another, by overriding the differences between them. It may sound paradoxical to stress in this way the differences within classes instead of those between classes. But I believe it is salutary to do so. If you take in turn the class

[1] From *The Social Sciences: their Relations in Theory and in Teaching*, 3rd ser. (Le Play House Press, 1938).

114

criteria that we have already discussed, income, property, education and occupation, you will find that every class contains within itself persons differently endowed in respect of each one of them. But the institution of class teaches the members of a society to notice some differences and to ignore others when arranging persons in order of social merit. In a word, social classes could not exist unless certain inequalities were regarded as irrelevant to the determination of social status. It follows that there are two main roads to the classless society. One leads through the abolition (as far as possible) of the social differences between individuals—which is roughly the way of communism—and the other proceeds by rendering all differences irrelevant to social status—which is roughly the way of democracy.

It is, of course, equally true that a class system notices, and even emphasises, certain forms of inequality, and uses them as a barrier to divide the classes. With respect to the points thus selected for attention members of the same class *are*—or believe they are—identical. But it is important to remember that they always differ in other respects. It is futile to argue that, because groups within a class are unlike in their circumstances or their interests, therefore the class itself is an 'artificial' group, or that because there is conflict within a class, therefore conflict between classes is 'unreal'.[1]

[1] Such words have only a relative meaning. All group attitudes must be based, not only on facts, but also on the social meaning given to them. An attitude is only 'unreal' if the meaning is excessively far-fetched or if, as in some types of propaganda, it is based on deliberate misrepresentation.

Antagonism, as Delevsky has argued at unnecessary length, is relative.[1] Those who are antagonists for one purpose may be colleagues for another. Our first task, then, is to classify the main forms of antagonism, in order to see which are most compatible with co-operation in other fields. The analysis will be confined to the types most important in the study of class conflict.

First, there is competition, where two or more persons offer the same service or desire the same object. This shows us at once that we cannot group people according to their resemblance to one another. In the case of competition it is similarity that divides; but let the competitors become partners, and the very same similarity will prove to be a bond of union. Secondly, there is the conflict that arises out of the division of labour, conflict, that is to say, over the terms on which co-operation is to take place, as illustrated by a wage dispute between employer and employed. The division here is a secondary product of a unity of interest based on difference. Thirdly, there is conflict over the system itself upon which the allocation of functions and the distribution of benefits are based, as when a bargain about wages is converted into a revolt against capitalism.

Antagonism between competitors is clearly not incompatible with a community of interest between them. In fact such a community of interest is implied in the term 'competition'. For competition is a social process conducted through the medium of institutions which are equally indispensable to both competitors. The very

[1] J. Delevsky, *Antagonismes sociaux et antagonismes prolétariens.*

existence of the service that is offered and its value in exchange are due to a social system and a civilisation that are a common possession. The power of this common interest to produce common action will vary according to circumstances, but the interest always exists. In the second type of antagonism co-operation between the antagonists is part of the definition. It is sometimes suggested that the co-existence of the two relationships is illusory, on the grounds that the antagonism is not real and that the true interests of the parties are identical. But this is absurd. It is true that he who drives a hard bargain may injure himself by ruining his opposite. Nevertheless, a bargain is in essence a wrangle within limits set by the need to continue the offer of the service bargained for. There is no more difficulty in admitting that buyer and seller are at the same time friends and enemies than in asserting that bowler and batsman have a common interest in helping one another to play cricket, although their views as to the most desirable fate of each ball bowled are diametrically opposed. More important is the question how far co-operation between, say, employer and employed is an obstacle to the solidarity of labour *vis-à-vis* capital. That it *is* an obstacle is obvious, but this does not mean that it is the more real interest of the two. Here again we have the fact that labour is united by its common position in relation to the institutions through which the bargain of co-operation takes place. And to this I would add that, whereas the co-operative function of production by division of labour is sectional and specialised, the antagonism which is inherent in every bargain expresses itself in terms which are general to the class, in terms of wages and hours and the basic conditions of bargaining power.

To sum up: competition within the ranks of labour (or capital) does not render impossible or unnatural a conscious unity of labour (or capital), and sectional co-operation between labour and capital does not render impossible or unnatural a general antagonism between labour and capital.[1]

It is only in the third type of conflict that the common interest shared by the rivals dwindles to vanishing point. In extreme cases conflict of this kind becomes civil war, which is not a social process and in which, as the world knows only too well, little regard is paid even to the accepted rules of warfare. I suggest that we might well reserve the term 'conflict' for cases in which the presence of this last type of antagonism can be detected. Neither competition nor bargaining is conflict in this refined sense, but when either party feels that the process of competing or bargaining ought not to take place at all, or that it is of necessity being conducted under conditions of injustice, then conflict appears and may grow to revolution. Conflict therefore, implies, not merely disagreement as to what is to be done next, but dissatisfaction with what already exists. Two parties in parliament disagree as to policy, but conflict begins when one denounces parliamentary government. Two parents may disagree about the education of their child, but conflict begins when the father denies that the mother has any say in the matter and the mother replies, 'I wish I had never married you.' And feelings of this kind may run as an undercurrent in the

[1] For an opposite view, see L. von Mises, *Socialism*, pt. III, § 1, ch. 4.

stream of disagreement for a long time before conflict breaks out, as has happened more than once in the history of trade unionism.[1]

I have been speaking so far, not about social classes, but about economic groups. I do not believe that the two are the same. I do believe in the reality of those social levels, distinguished by their culture and standard of living, which we discussed at our first two meetings. But differences of level are less likely to lead to conflict than differences of group interest. To that extent I accept the Marxian analysis of the nature of class conflict (though not the theory of its historic role), but I deny that it exhausts the subject of social stratification. Simplifying for the sake of brevity, I should say that class conflict occurs when a common interest unites adjacent social levels in opposition to more distant social levels. When the levels united by a common interest are not adjacent, as in international war, the conflict is not a class conflict. The fusion of levels is facilitated when the divisions between them are of unequal depth, when, for instance, the gulfs between levels one to four are shallower than that between levels four and five. There is another cause of fusion. Class conflict arises over social institutions. Often the same institutions dominate the division into levels. In such cases the two types of cleavage play into one another's hands. I imagine this was the case in feudal society. It is arguable that it is less true to-day. The wage-earner with savings finds that his social level

[1] The General Strike showed well what confusion of mind results when the forms of bargaining are used for the purposes of conflict.

urges him to defend the rights of property while his interests as a wage-earner prompt him to invade them. The issue depends partly on the nature of the conflict of interests, and on this point the analysis can be carried a stage further.

That resentment against inequality which is characteristic of class antagonism may spring from three processes, which I shall call comparison, frustration and oppression. Comparison sustains both the sense of superiority of the rich over 'the great unwashed' and the sense of resentment in the poor against 'the idle rich'. Such feelings may be shared by any number of persons from a single individual to a whole nation, and they are therefore most uncertain in their group-making effects. Yet they are the main force creating social levels, and they do this, not so much by provoking antagonism, as by perfecting the individual's awareness of himself and the group's consciousness of its own character. They are foundations of self-esteem. Perhaps that is why men seem to prefer to concentrate on comparing themselves with their inferiors. It is said that there is no caste in India so low that it cannot point to another beneath it. Comparison does not make contacts, it breaks them. It leads to isolation rather than to conflict. But if conflict is brewing, the attitudes born of comparison will stimulate it, and, when it matures, embitter it, and they are always there, ready to convert into a class struggle a dispute which is in essence no more than a disagreement about the terms of co-operation.[1]

[1] Subject, of course, to the reservations made above about the effect of social levels on class unity.

Frustration adds to comparison a stronger motive for conflict by definitely imputing to the superior class responsibility for the injustice under which the inferior suffers. It arises, of course, wherever privilege creates inequality of opportunity. But more important, because more distinctive, is the case where two classes represent, as it were, two different economic systems or two incompatible conceptions of social life. Pirenne has suggested that this is the normal way of economic progress. The creators of the new order rise up alongside of, not among, the decaying champions of the old.[1] The result is a lateral conflict, in which the old order appears more as an obstacle than as a tyrant. The process can be seen most clearly in the history of the bourgeoisie from the beginnings of the decline of feudalism to the perfection of capitalism in the nineteenth century, and especially in France. In the early days, says Pirenne, the bourgeois 'merely desired a place in the sun, and their claims were confined to their most indispensable needs'.[2] Subsequently it became clearer that concessions to the bourgeois involved sacrifices by the aristocrat. Later, says Henri Sée, the bourgeoisie 'a intérêt au nouvel ordre de choses, à une organisation plus régulière, à la destruction des privilèges des deux premiers ordres, à la reconnaissance de l'égalité civile'.[3] Privilege was an obstacle because it was a cause of administrative inefficiency and financial mismanagement. How confused were ideas at the time

---

[1] *Les périodes de l'histoire sociale du capitalisme.*
[2] *Economic and social history of medieval Europe,* p. 51.
[3] *La vie économique au xviii⁴ siècle,* p. 173.

of the Fronde as to the relations between social strata appears from the fact that the government's first act, when it realised the danger of disturbance, was to call on the bourgeois militia to stand by, while the revolutionary bourgeoisie organised a mercenary army of *compagnons* to relieve their portly selves of the burden of drilling and carrying arms.[1]

It might be argued that the position to-day is similar. The new middle class, composed mainly of the salariat and the lesser professions, is not writhing under the heel of a tyrant, but it is uncomfortably aware that the realisation of its great ideal of a quiet life lived in security and with full enjoyment of the arts of civilisation is being prevented by the incessant wranglings of capital and labour, which seem to it to be an essential part of the social system of the last century, and by the obsession of men's minds by a restless longing to speculate and to bargain in a ceaseless striving for profits. Either capitalism or socialism alone would be preferable, because both must use the services of this middle class in much the same way. But the conflict between the two is enough to goad it into revolution, with the natural, though not entirely wished-for, result of Fascist dictatorship. Conflict against frustration is likely to include moral denunciation of the old order as corrupt, perverted or decadent. The modern middle-class movement shows this strain. It denounces materialism and the lack of a sense of social brotherhood, and, perhaps, the failure to appreciate the

[1] Charles Normand, *La bourgeoisie française au xviiᵉ siècle*, p. 349. In general see Joseph Aynard, *La bourgeoisie française*, chs. 8 and 9.

value of the artists and intellectuals. Fascism offers a new mind and a new spirit. 'The Fascist State...is a force, but a spiritual force, which embodies in itself all forms of the moral and intellectual life of man.... Its principle...implants itself in the heart of the man of action, the thinker, the artist and the scientist alike— it is the soul of the soul.'[1] This is not exactly what was asked for, but it may serve for a time.

Oppression describes a conflict between two parties engaged in unequal co-operation, the inequality being a product of the institutions of a stratified society. The word is not meant to define the motives or methods of the upper class, but only the situation as it appears to the lower. Whereas comparison breaks contacts and frustration produces contact by collision, oppression implies contact as an organic process. Obvious instances are the relations between serf and lord or labour and capital. When conflict breaks out, the attack is made against a group of persons wielding power. They may be referred to as 'the governing class'. This phrase is loosely used. The feudal aristocracy was literally a governing class. The modern capitalists are not. And yet the words express a truth. The implication is that the capitalist is using in the economic field a power that is partly political, in that it is derived from the laws and institutions of the society. If a class is strong enough to secure or to preserve those institutions that favour its activities, it may be said to be 'governing' to that extent. But, as we saw, in the modern world interest in the essential institutions is

[1] B. Mussolini, *La dottrina del Fascismo*, § 12.

not confined to the capitalists who meet labour as employers. It is perhaps for this reason that the attack comes to be directed less against a group of persons than against an impersonal system. Relations between the co-operating groups relapse into bargaining. Conflict deals in theories. One would expect this to result in a decline in the influence of trade unionists, who bargain, as leaders of a working class, in favour of communists, who theorise. An alternative consequence may be an increase in what might be called 'level-consciousness' as compared with 'class-consciousness'. This seems to be what is happening in England.

Space remains for only one more point. We can ask whether conflict is more likely to arise in a static or a dynamic society. This involves contrasting estate with class, status with contract. In a society stratified into estates inequality is based on an accepted scheme of differential status and differential standards of living. One class is utilised for the benefit of another, but within the limits of a plan of co-operation approved by custom. Disagreement over the terms of co-operation can hardly arise, since the terms are not open to question. Where status rules, bargaining, which belongs to contract, cannot prevail. Antagonism can find no expression except in conflict.[1] There is no middle course between acquiescence and rebellion. It might be argued that this must render conflict more likely, because there is no milder alternative. But it may equally be urged that the gravity of the step

[1] Cf. K. Bauer-Mengelberg, 'Stand und Klasse', in *Kölner Vierteljahrshefte für Soziologie* (1923).

will act as a deterrent. It is easier to drift into danger than to jump into it. In addition, the very nature of a society based on estates is such as to favour the development in each group of the type of mentality suited to its position. Revolt is paralysed from within.

In a free contractual society disagreement as to the terms of co-operation is normal and chronic. It is implied in the bargaining process out of which the contract emerges. We notice, too, that the idea that every station in life has its proper standard, that every class has its culture, is at the weakest. Acquiescence is positively discouraged by the prevailing belief in the virtue of social ambition. Democracy professes to believe in equality and capitalism extols competition. A uniform standard for all kills competition, while differential standards deny equality. Capitalist democracy, therefore, at first accepts no standard, taking what is given it by the free play of economic forces. The English pauper was not to be fed according to the needs of the human body but according to what could be bought with a little less money than capitalism vouchsafed to the free worker. When the standard enters once more, as it did in the later nineteenth century, it enters as a minimum, above which infinite variation is allowed and expected. In capitalist democracy, then, we have a perpetual state of friction between classes combined with a destruction of the psychological forces favouring acquiescence. Is there, we should ask, any positive force turning antagonism into conflict which is absent in the static society? I see a possible answer in the idea of exploitation.

In both types of society there appears to be utilisation of one class by another for the benefit of the latter. But whereas in the society of estates it is according to plan, in the contractual society it is at will. To distinguish between these processes we may say that the second is exploitation and the first is not. The benefits accruing to lord and serf under feudalism cannot be compared, because they are different in kind. Those accruing to capital and labour seem to be measured by their money incomes, and they are manifestly unequal. A contract is ideally an agreement to co-operate for equal advantage. When it habitually produces unequal advantage, exploitation is suspected. The idea appeals strongly to the exploited, who quickly conclude that the power that is defeating them resides, not in the personal superiority of their oppressor, but in the unfair advantages he derives from the system. If the system renders contract a sham, the system must be changed.

Some people hold that social mobility affords a safety-valve and helps to avert the threatened conflict. Although this is true up to a point, I think its importance can easily be exaggerated. Where individual mobility is automatic, or nearly so, class loyalty develops with difficulty. If every apprentice has a reasonable hope of becoming a master he will form his associations on the basis of his trade or profession rather than of his social level. Again, where a whole group can rise in social estimation and economic value, leaving no stragglers, the alliance of groups into classes is more difficult. This is no doubt the effect of the recent rise of many skilled occupations into the ranks of the professions. But where mobility is individual and not automatic, but depends on the results of competitive striving, I am doubtful whether the same result follows. When the race is to the swift, the slow, who are always in a majority, grow tired of their perpetual defeat and become more disgruntled than if there were no race at all. They begin to regard the prizes as something to which they are entitled and of which they are unjustly deprived. They declare that no man ought to be made to race for his bread and butter, and the argument is not without force. Especially is this so when society shows itself indifferent to the condition of the losers on the ground that the road to better things is ever open before them.[1] The use of mobility as an excuse for inequality is usually associated with a measure of self-deception. But, if I were to pursue that theme, I should be trespassing on the subject to be discussed at the next session of this Conference.

[1] Cf. C. H. Cooley, *Social Organization*, ch. 27.

(IV)

THE RECENT HISTORY OF PROFESSIONALISM IN RELATION TO SOCIAL STRUCTURE AND SOCIAL POLICY[1]

THE professions, conceived as a select body of superior occupations, have existed from time immemorial, although their identity has often been in dispute. The ancients wrote and argued about them,[2] while Herbert Spencer traced their origin among primitive peoples.[3] The earliest view to which we need here pay attention was that occupations should be judged and valued according to their compatibility with the good life. They were to be tested by their effect on the giver of the service rather than on the recipient. The professions were, in English parlance, the occupations suitable for a gentleman. This idea naturally flourished in societies which distinguished sharply between life lived as an end in itself, and life passed in providing the means which enable others to live as free civilised men should. The professions in such a society were those means to living which were most innocuous, in that they did not dull the brain, like manual labour, nor

[1] From *The Canadian Journal of Economics and Political Science*, vol. 5, no. 3, August 1939 (University of Toronto Press).
[2] See, for example, Otto Neurath, 'Zur Anschauung der Antike über Handel, Gewerbe und Landwirtschaft', in *Jahrbücher für National-ökonomie und Statistik* (Jena, 1906, vol. LXXXVII, p. 577).
[3] *The Principles of Sociology* (London, 1896), vol. III, pt. VII.

corrupt the soul, like commerce. They even contained within themselves qualities and virtues which might well find a place among the ends of the good life itself. Leisure, based on the ownership of land or of slaves, was the chief mark of aristocracy, and here too the professions were but slightly inferior. For leisure does not mean idleness. It means the freedom to choose your activities according to your own preferences and your own standards of what is best. The professions, it was said, enjoyed this kind of freedom, not so much because they were free from the control of an employer—that was assumed—but rather because, for them, choice was not restricted and confined by economic pressure. The professional man, it has been said, does not work in order to be paid: he is paid in order that he may work. Every decision he takes in the course of his career is based on his sense of what is right, not on his estimate of what is profitable. That, at least, is the impression he would like to create when defending his claim to superior status.

This position was a difficult one for the professions to maintain. Their dilemma was indicated by Adam Smith. 'We trust our health to the physician,' he wrote, 'our fortune and sometimes our life and reputation to the lawyer and attorney. Such confidence could not safely be reposed in people of a very mean or low condition. Their reward must be such, therefore, as may give them that rank in the society which so important a trust requires.'[1] The professions, in other words, are respectable

---

[1] *An Inquiry into the Nature and Causes of the Wealth of Nations*, edited by Edwin Cannan, 5th ed. (London, 1930), vol. I, p. 107.

because they do not strive for money, but they can only remain respectable if they succeed, in spite of this pecuniary indifference, in making quite a lot of money, enough for the needs of a gentlemanly life. Money must flow in as an almost unsolicited recognition of their inestimable services. Nor did Adam Smith make things any easier for them by classing them as 'unproductive labour', a judgement with which many ordinary men and women, when faced with the necessity of employing a lawyer, are only too prone to concur.

But conditions have changed since then. Leisure is no longer in the same sense the mark of aristocracy, and commerce is no longer a disreputable occupation. Leisure is, of course, still important as a determinant of social status, but instead of describing a spiritual quality of freedom that pervades the whole of one's activities, it means merely the way one spends one's money when the day's work is done. The way the money is earned is increasingly unimportant. It is the quantity that matters. The business man's leisure is as good as anyone else's, because leisure is simply the antithesis to work.[1] And in addition he can pay apparent homage to the older ideas by purchasing complete idleness for his wife, and by himself becoming a complete and genuine gentleman of leisure when he retires from business. The professional man had to change his ground. He had to admit that his occupation was laborious, like the tradesman's—and even to glory in the fact—but to assert that it was labour of a special and superior kind. In defining

[1] See H. V. Durant, *The Problem of Leisure* (London, 1938), ch. 1.

its peculiar character the emphasis was shifted from the effect of the service on the giver to that on the recipient, or, more accurately, to the relationship between the two. The idea of service became more important than the idea of freedom. Certain professional types, representing the old view in its extreme form, grew more scarce and are now almost extinct: for example, the man of good family but insufficient means who occupied a sinecure in the service of the State; the humbler member of a similar stock, ill-endowed with brains and character, who drifted through the Civil Service leaving little impression of his passage; the hunting parson and the wealthy ecclesiastical pluralist; the young aristocrat who entered the army as a pastime rather than as a career; the scholar who regarded pupils as intruders disturbing the peace of his academic life; the schoolmaster who felt that he had fully discharged his duties by being a gentleman and a sportsman—a type of which some examples may still be found in England to-day. There was no honourable place for these in the strenuous and efficient life of the nineteenth century. Even in medicine, where the value of training and hard work is most obvious, the standard of scientific qualifications had declined as the profession became recognised as a gateway to social prestige and opportunity. Carr-Saunders, referring to conditions in England in the eighteenth century, writes: 'The physicians had long established themselves in the upper ranks of society, and when scientific enquiry lost its novelty, they joined in the ample life of the great houses where elegance and wit were pursued.... Social qualifications became the first requirement for membership [of the College of Physicians], and it was held that the necessary "morals and manners" could be learnt only at the universities.[1] With the foundation of the British Medical Association in 1856 and of the General Medical Council in 1858 this period of lassitude came to an end.

There can be no doubt that, in mid-Victorian England, the professions were prosperous and respected, and they owed their position mainly to the work of the professional associations. The principles of their policy are familiar, and there is no space in this paper to go into detail. In the first place the association guarantees the technical effciency of its members, not by supervising their work, but by testing their ability before they are admitted to practise. This involves an indirect control of their training. Secondly, it imposes a code of ethics which includes the duty to offer service whenever and wherever it is required, to give only the best, to abstain from competition, advertisement, and all commercial haggling, and to respect the confidence of the client. Thirdly, it does what it can to protect its field from invasion by the unqualified—that is, it enjoys a partial monopoly—and to keep up the standard of remuneration of its members, and in general to safeguard the conditions of their work.

It can be argued that all this insistence on service and on ethical obligations is a mere camouflage to disguise the purely selfish desire to create an artificial scarcity and to win the material and immaterial advantages which scarcity can confer. I do not propose to deal directly with the

[1] A. M. Carr-Saunders and P. A. Wilson, *The Professions* (Oxford, 1933), p. 71.

evidence for and against this view, but to approach the subject indirectly by asking whether the ethical code is an arbitrary fabrication of the professional mind or whether it reflects some real characteristics which distinguish the professions from the trades.

Ethical codes are based on the belief that between professional and client there is a relationship of trust, and between buyer and seller there is not. In so far as the professions purvey services and the trades commodities, the difference is obvious. The commodity can be inspected before it is paid for: the service cannot. The principle of *caveat emptor* is at least plausible when you are buying a horse or a pound of strawberries: it makes nonsense when you are calling in a surgeon to a case of acute appendicitis. But there is more to it than that. Many services can be satisfactorily controlled by commercial contracts. Some of them, like those of the builder or the tailor, lead to the production of a commodity which can be judged by objective tests and rejected if it is not according to specification. But if you engage an artist to paint your portrait, you must accept—and pay for— whatever he produces. If he says it is his finest work, you are in no position to contradict him. Other services are so standardised and impersonal that they can be exactly measured and defective work can be penalised. Where labour is employed in the mass on a man-week basis, any failure of an individual workman to come up to expectations is quickly remedied, without serious loss, by dismissal. Standardised labour, in fact, can be treated as a commodity. But with the professions it is otherwise.

133

It is beyond the wit of man to devise a contract that would specify, in terms that could be enforced, what it is that the client expects to receive.

There are two reasons for this. One is that professional service is not standardised. It is unique and personal. But that is true to some extent of all skilled labour. The professional man is distinguished by the further fact that he does not give only his skill. He gives himself. His whole personality enters into his work. It is hardly possible to be satisfied with a doctor or a lawyer unless one likes and respects him as a man. He is called upon to show judgement and an understanding of human nature, as well as a knowledge of medicine or law. The best service can be given only when the practitioner knows his client intimately, his character, his foibles, his background, and his family circumstances. That is why the British Medical Association is now deploring the way in which specialisation and institutional treatment are ousting the family doctor from his key position. These essential qualities cannot be specified in a contract, they cannot be bought. They can only be given. The clients trust to professional traditions and professional ethics to develop and train those qualities and make them available for the service of the public. The mistrust of women doctors, which is not yet quite overcome, was probably due to the feeling that they had not had the chance to imbibe these traditions. During their training they were kept on the fringes of the medical community, while, in addition, the influences of home and school, which had long been directed to producing in boys the virtues demanded by the codes of professional ethics, had ignored the girls or even fostered in them quite different qualities. Any member of the working class who aspires to professional status has to fight against the same difficulties and the same suspicions.

With art, which is also classed among the professions, the case is different. The artist, too, cannot labour in a detached, impersonal way, with his eye on the clock and his mind on his cheque. He, too, must give something that is deeply rooted in his nature, something that cannot be commanded or coerced, or even bribed. But with him it is not his human judgement, his probity, his sound knowledge of life and affairs. It is his creative genius. The attitude of the client to the lawyer is roughly this. 'I am asking you', he says, 'to act as my brain in this matter. I want you to think and judge for me, because I haven't the technical equipment to think and judge for myself. But please do so exactly as I should if I knew the law.' The lawyer, therefore—and I am thinking here of the solicitor rather than the barrister—must have the qualities of the ordinary man undiluted by the ordinary weaknesses. He must be a model of the unshakable middle-class virtues. Eccentricity is fatal, and his private life must be beyond reproach. The artist, on the other hand, is valued because he is different, peculiar. He has the spark that is lacking in the composition of the ordinary man. Eccentricity is an asset. He can thrive on scandal. But the principle of the relationship is the same, for in both cases the professional must be trusted to give what he cannot be compelled or contractually bound to give.

The second reason for the relationship of trust has already been hinted at. It is the ignorance of the client. He often hardly knows what to ask for, let alone how it can be provided. He must surrender all initiative and put himself in his lawyer's hands or under his doctor's orders. That is the great difference between the services of professionals and the services of wage-earners or salaried employees. Authority passes from buyer to seller. It is true that the modern salesman tries to use authority, but with a difference. When the doctor says, 'Take more exercise', it is a command. When the associated greengrocers plaster the hoardings with the slogan, 'Eat more fruit', it is an effort at mass suggestion.

One crucial point has still to be considered before we can sum up this part of the argument, and that is the balance between the duty to the client and the duty to the community. The relationship of trust implies a deep obligation to the client. But an organised profession rightly regards itself as a body placed in charge of an art or science and responsible for directing its use in the interests of society. These two obligations can be reconciled without difficulty if the true interests of society and of the individual are harmonious. A profession proceeds on the assumption that they are. When they seem to be in conflict it is usually because the individual does not know what is good for him. The client, as we have seen, is often ignorant. Authority passes to the professional, who must give him what he needs, rather than what he wants. The client, unlike the customer, is not always right. The guilty criminal wants an acquittal, but what he needs, and what his lawyer must give him, is a fair trial. Now need is a social concept. It can only be assessed in relation to the social order within which the individual is living, and in assessing it the professional must draw on standards that are within his own mind and conscience, placed there by his training and his traditions. Sometimes the State solves his problem by issuing a precise order, as when it forbids a doctor to procure an abortion on an unwilling mother who is physically capable of bearing a child without risk to herself. Sometimes the profession lays down a rule. But often the professional must judge for himself, as when a painter refuses to prostitute his art to the bad taste of the public.

The professions have not always lived up to these high ideals. They have not always struck a true balance between loyalty to the client and loyalty to the community, and they have sometimes treated loyalty to the profession as an end rather than as a means to the fulfilment of the other loyalties. They are often accused of neglecting the public welfare. Doctors, it is said, showed too little interest in public health, architects in town planning, scholars in general education, and artists in the culture of the masses. These are sins of omission. ·Against the lawyers the graver charge has been made that they used their position to defeat the real intentions of the law in order to benefit their clients and themselves. American lawyers, said Theodore Roosevelt, made 'it their special task to work out bold and ingenious schemes by which their wealthy clients, individual and corporate, can evade the laws which were made to regulate, in the interests of the public, the uses of wealth'.¹ There have been many other statements in the same sense, especially, though not exclusively, with reference to lawyers in the United States. Sometimes, how-ever, the charge is found, on examination, to be, not that lawyers have frustrated the law, but that they have worked to maintain a legal system of which the critic disapproves.

The position of the professions in the recent past was a curious one. They enjoyed, as organisations, varying degrees of group monopoly and developed, in varying degrees, a group spirit and a group conscience. And yet their general attitude was one of intense individualism, which made them unsympathetic, or at least indifferent, to social planning. But they evinced strong disapproval of competition and unrestricted self-seeking among their members. In estimating the significance of this position it is important to discover the true balance between its individualist and corporate elements. Professor Laski, in a recent article, has laid the main weight on the former. 'The individualistic organisation of these professions', he writes, 'is now fatal to the fulfilment of their function. They cannot, I shall argue, give of their best to the civil-isation in which they play so large a part so long as their members offer their services for private hire and sale.... In the present state of civilisation the prospect of their ful-filling their end as a profession declines rather than grows.'² This suggests that, so long as the professional works

---

¹ William Durran, *The Lawyer, Our Old-man-of-the-sea* (London, 1913), p. 50.
² 'The Decline of the Professions', in *Harper's Monthly Magazine*, November 1935, pp. 656–7.

on his own for fees paid directly by his clients, his pecuniary interests will prevent him from fulfilling his social obligations, whatever professional associations may do, through their ethical codes, to curb the profit motive in their members.

First let us be clear what these codes imply. They do not assert that a professional man should be indifferent to money and unambitious to extend his practice and increase his income. They assert only that he must do this legitimately, without impairing the quality of his work or withholding those extra personal services which cannot be specifically demanded by the client and are not specifically paid for. Now, the facts do not suggest that this ideal is unattainable while professional men continue in private practice. The cases most commonly cited as evidence of failure are those of the fashionable medical specialist and the successful barrister. The charge has foundation. The opportunities for money-making in such positions are great enough to tempt some to deviate from strict professional standards. But it should be noticed that the specialist differs from the general practitioner and the barrister from the solicitor precisely on the point that they never establish that close relationship with the client that is the foundation of true professionalism. They are called in *to* a case rather than *by* a client, and the medical profession, at least, is fully alive to the dangers involved. Of the professions as a whole one could not fairly say what Veblen said of business men, that they care only for the vendibility of their product, and not at all for its serviceability.

139

But individualism may have another foundation, not related to private pecuniary gain. It may mean the belief that the individual is the true unit of service, because service depends on individual qualities and individual judgement, supported by an individual responsibility which cannot be shifted on to the shoulders of others. That, I believe, is the essence of professionalism, and it is not concerned with self-interest, but with the welfare of the client. And this welfare, as I have said, is, and must be, conceived in social terms, even when clients are dealt with one by one as separate units. There is no need to abandon this kind of individualism when the service is offered to a group or to a community. In this sense of the word a prime minister is an individualist, so is a judge or a general in command of an army, and so, too, is any subordinate who clings to the divine right of disobedience. There is nothing in this attitude fundamentally antagonistic to public service or social planning. As one speaker put it at the last conference of the British Medical Association, when discussing the distinction between the private and public medical services: 'The difference was that the medical officer as commonly understood aimed at individual health through communal health, and the general practitioner at communal health through individual health.'[1] They are natural allies, with a common objective, but circumstances have, in the past, been unfavourable to the development of the alliance. There are two main reasons for this. One is a very natural fear of State control. The profession claims to be judge in its own

[1] *British Medical Journal* (Supplement), 13 August 1938, p. 367.

cause. Once the State assumes control it can dictate the standards of service, and enslave the collective conscience of the profession. This means much more than the mere disposal of labour, because, as we saw, the labour of the professional is inseparable from the man. It is no idle fear. Churches have had to fight for religious liberty and universities for academic freedom. Professor Laski urges that the legal profession 'should be a great corporation under government control', as it is in Soviet Russia. But under Hitler, he says, 'a body of learned professors, whose vocation was the disinterested service of truth, were there willing to prostitute their scholarship to ends which hundreds of them knew to be mean and false'.[1] His view appears to be that the State should control the professions, but that the professions should at the same time control the State. And that is not easy, unless State and professions are agreed on the fundamentals of policy.

The second reason for professional individualism is simply this. The professional man cannot spread his services, he cannot, except within narrow limits, distribute his skill through subordinates. He is unable to go in for mass production and is forbidden to offer cheap lines for slender purses. Since he works for a limited market it is not surprising that he should choose one which is solvent and concentrate on the wealthy individual client. In other words, he must find an employer, and the general public was not organised for his employment. The doctors, whose sense of public duty has always been strong, got

[1] 'The Decline of the Professions', *ib.* p. 684.

round this difficulty to a large extent by giving free service to the poor while living on fees taken from the rich, and by organising unofficial insurance schemes in country districts under which the villager paid his penny a week while he was well and received the attendance he needed when he was ill. But speaking generally this state of affairs led to a maldistribution of professional services in terms of social need, a maldistribution due to economic motives among professional men but not necessarily implying any disloyalty to the principle that service must not be sacrificed to profit. It was this, no doubt, that Professor Laski had chiefly in mind. Big-scale social activities only became possible when the initiative was taken by the State and the local authorities, by public corporations and rich charities. And by that time the professions had built up their tradition of individualism, which meant not so much the pursuit of individual self-interest as the service of individual clients in a relationship of individual trust. They were therefore disinclined to press for the establishment of corporate agencies for the distribution of professional services and reluctant to work for them when they appeared. But time has wrought a change. There has been a silent revolution in the social services to which the professions are adapting themselves. It is not a painful process, because the adaptation does not involve a surrender of any of the fundamentals of the professional ideal. In my brief description of this change I shall be speaking of recent events in Britain.

The social services were at first directed to the relief of extreme poverty and extreme distress by provision of the minimum necessary for a decent life. What they gave was much what was given by low-grade private enterprise. They did not look at social problems in a new or original way. Inferior quality was implicit in the idea that they were acts of charity to human failures and that they must do nothing to weaken the incentive to self-help. The professions were not expected to be interested in supplying cheap lodging-houses, cheap medicines, or cheap education to the indigent. As the political system became more democratic the sense of responsibility for social welfare grew stronger. Public health led the way, because it was soon compelled to treat the environment and not merely the individual. That meant a service to the community and not merely to a class. Gradually the Poor Law Infirmaries are being absorbed into the general hospital system, while medical services, under the National Health Insurance scheme, are extended to the whole of the employed working class and will soon, without doubt, spread further up the social scale. The education authorities came to realise that, even if they provided only an elementary education, it must be the best possible, since they were catering for the vast majority of the children of the nation. Charity schools for the poor belonged to the remote past. Then secondary and technical education were brought within the scope of public enterprise, and through these schools working-class children could pass into State-aided universities. The meagre provision of working-class dwellings grew into slum clearance, town planning, and regional planning.

The story is too long to be told and too familiar to need

telling. The essential point is that the social services have grown from a cheap make-shift provided for the lowest class in a society that built on competitive individualism, into a vast co-ordinated plan for the betterment of the entire community. The social services have lost, or are rapidly losing, their class character. They are inspired by the spirit of professionalism, in the sense that they do not design their work to meet an articulate and effective demand only, but plan it in the light of expert knowledge of the social arts and sciences and of fundamental principles of social welfare formulated on the basis of accumulated human experience. The authority exercised by the social services differs from that of the professions. It rests not only on the superior knowledge of the administrators but also on political power derived from the constitution. A relationship of trust is essential, but it is founded on the principles of political obligation, not on private honour and a traditional ethic.

A vast army of professional men and women is employed in these services without losing professional status, and many more co-operate without becoming employees of the government. There would seem at first sight to be two main differences between these agents of the social services and the independent professions. In the first place they are working for an employer. But if that were reckoned as unprofessional, one would have to strike many of the oldest and most honoured professions off the list: the fighting forces, public administration, the teachers and many engineers, scientists, artists, and writers. Secondly they are working for the community and not for individual clients. But this, it has already been argued, is a difference of form rather than of essence.

Admittedly the situation is dangerous when a free profession must work under the orders of a superior. The commands of the superior may clash with the conscience of the profession, and this is particularly serious when the commands are backed by the unlimited power of the State. But I believe that in modern democratic societies this danger is diminishing rather than increasing, because State and professions are being assimilated to one another. This is not happening through the absorption of the professions by the State, but by both of them moving from opposite directions to meet in a middle position. The natural foe of professionalism in private life is commercialism. Its natural foe in public life is politics, in the less reputable sense of that term. Both bring in extraneous motives and scales of value inappropriate to the real business in hand. Now it is a commonplace that the growing technical complexity of the public services is shifting the balance of power from the politician to the administrator. The British social services are not yet above, or beyond, politics, but they are moving in that direction, and other democratic countries are likely in time to follow in the same path. Political controversy still rages over broad proposals for reform and over some provocative details, but there are wide areas of action left to the administrators and the professionals where the voice of the politician is but dimly heard as the distant

ineffectual bleating of a wandering sheep. Within that
field a clash of ideals is unlikely. Co-operation is close
and friendly, and this, in Britain, is largely due to the
professional character of the Civil Service. Civil servants
are not commercially minded, and politically they are
passive. In the past it was said that this left them spiritu-
ally eviscerated; they were reduced to a collection of
type-writers, calculating machines, and rubber stamps
actuated by a plausible imitation of human vitality. That
is not, and could not any longer be true, because the
Civil Service is no longer merely an administrative body.
In much of his work, as Dr Robson has put it, 'the official
is less concerned to administer the law than to promote
energetic and far-reaching projects based on plans which
he himself must create'.[1] These projects are preceded by
thorough inquiries and investigations, in which outside
professional help is enlisted through those invaluable
institutions, the Departmental Committee and the Royal
Commission, and in many other more permanent ways.
The quality of official reports is now so high that most of
them could pass the severest academic tests that a university could impose, because they are the fruit of the
same professional spirit that inspires the work of the
universities themselves. If this were not so, it would be
a pure farce to ask a commission to investigate the causes
of the present distribution of the industrial population and
the probable direction of future change, and to report on
the social, economic, and strategical disadvantages of

[1] *The British Civil Servant*, edited by W. A. Robson (London, 1937),
p. 19.

concentration in particular areas.[1] A great exploratory inquiry of that kind is neither a political nor an administrative act. It is a piece of big-scale social research.

In short, the professions are being socialised and the social and public services are being professionalised. The professions are learning, not merely to recognise their obligations to society as a whole as well as those to individual clients, but also to break down the traditional isolation which separated them from one another. They are ready to work as a team. In fact the value of team work was probably realised earlier in the public services than in the fields of academic social research, where it is just as necessary. A recent report issued by the British Ministry of Health opened with the following striking passage: 'The skill and experience of the physician, the surgeon, the obstetrician, the epidemiologist, the architect, the engineer, the lawyer, the statistician, the sociologist, the veterinary surgeon and the administrator have all been assembled to constitute the science of public health, which is thus a compendium of specialised knowledge.'[2] The list is long, but it could easily be doubled.

In the meantime the professions, in their independent capacity, were moving in a similar direction. One might refer to the artists, and cite their greater readiness to give serious attention to some of the more communal forms of

[1] Summary of the terms of reference of the Royal Commission on the Distribution of the Industrial Population, set up in July 1937.
[2] *Annual Report of the Chief Medical Officer of the Ministry of Health or 1937* (London, 1938), p. 1.

art, for the stage, for internal decoration, and even for commercial posters, and their highly successful efforts to raise the standard of art teaching in schools of every grade. One might mention the architects, who for the first time have had a chance of devoting their talents to designing homes for the people as well as residences for the rich and who have recently founded a School of Planning and Research in London in which to study the problems of the architect against the background of the social scene. One could claim that the teachers now realise more fully the dignity and the responsibilities of their calling and see themselves as the trustees of a national service instead of the bored drudges of an impersonal authority. Incidentally it is of interest that teachers and education officers up and down the country have voiced their condemnation of the latest Education Act, which raises the school-leaving age to fifteen but allows the release of a child for 'beneficial employment' at the age of fourteen. This is a case of professional standards being invoked to discredit the tricks of political manœuverers.

But the outstanding example is that of medicine. Many public utterances can be quoted to illustrate the changed attitude of the profession. Here is a simple one from Sir Kaye Le Fleming, spoken at the annual meeting of the British Medical Association last July. Our charge to our students, he said, should be as follows: 'When you go out into practice you have no right to sit alone in your own little niche seeing how much money you can make by attending patients who are ill. You will remember that you have duties to the profession as a whole, to the public as a whole and to the State.'[1] That is a straightforward denunciation of old-fashioned professional individualism. The next is bolder. It comes from the President's address to the same gathering. 'I have said that this is an age of youth. It is also an age of planning. *Laissez-faire*, that principle beloved of our fathers, has done great things but it has outlived its time. All the signs and symptoms point to the fact that, whether we wish it or not, in every field of human activity some form of control, of planning, is necessarily coming. We may not like the thought, but it is useless to kick against the pricks, and it rests largely with us what form that control is going to take.'[2]

There is some evidence that these are not mere empty words. For the new attitude towards medical service seems to grow naturally out of the new attitude towards health. In the British Medical Association's scheme for a General Medical Service for the Nation[3]—itself a sign of serious purpose—the first basic principle is 'that the system of medical service should be directed to the achievement of positive health and the prevention of disease no less than to the relief of sickness'. Positive health, according to Sir Henry Brackenbury, means 'not the absence of illness only, but an actual and definite sense of well-being', in pursuit of which medicine must aim at 'the constructive enhancement and perfecting of the communal and personal health'.[4] Positive health is not some-

[1] *British Medical Journal* (supplement), 13 August 1938, p. 368.
[2] *Ib.* 23 July 1938, p. 163.
[3] See the pamphlet with this title published by the Association in 1938.
[4] 'Medical Progress and Society', in *Human Affairs*, edited by R. B. Cattell, J. Cohen, and R. M. W. Travers (London, 1937), pp. 125–6.

thing clearly and specifically felt by the individual, something for which he can ask the doctor to prescribe in the way that he asks him to prescribe for a pain or a temperature. The ordinary man does not know the possibilities of health. And when positive health is thought of in terms of communal perfection it involves treatment not only of the physical but also of the social environment, a change, perhaps, in social habits, an education in the art of life. Positive health, in fact, is an ideal which can only be defined in relation to an ideal society. That may sound grandiloquent. But I am not professing to record an achievement. I am only trying to describe an aspiration.

It has not been my purpose in all this to whitewash the professions. Their faults and deficiencies have been legion. My aim has been to make three points. First, that professionalism is an idea based on the real character of certain services. It is not a clever invention of selfish minds. Secondly, the individualistic bias of the major professions was a product of circumstance. It was not the corner-stone of the building. Thirdly, the professions to-day are being weaned from this excessive individualism and are adapting themselves to the new standards of social service. The change has been stimulated by outside pressure, but the professions have made an independent contribution of their own and helped to build up the influences to which they themselves are in turn reacting.

There remains the topic of social structure referred to in the title of this paper, but there is time to treat it only in the broadest outline. The most obvious trend has been the weakening of aristocratic prejudices against trade and the consequent amalgamation of the upper levels in the worlds of business and the professions. But society is still somewhat fastidious in picking the commercial positions which it regards as gentlemanly, and it is noticeable that it prefers to bestow, for social purposes, the courtesy rank of professions on precisely those business careers that are furthest removed in character from the professional ideal, in that they are most completely devoted to money values, money profits, and speculation. If one were ruminating on the probable alignment of forces in case of a future crisis one would note these social affinities between the upper ranks of certain professions and of financial capitalism, and hazard a guess that capitalist interests would be the dominating influence in the group.

But at a lower social level the picture is different. Here the remarkable thing is the rapid spread of the forms of professional organisation among occupational groups which are not professions in the full meaning of the term. The forms which such groups can adopt are: recognised courses of training in a specialised technique, a means of testing efficiency in that technique, the admission of those duly qualified into an association, the building up of the prestige of the association as against non-members, the imposition of certain standards of honourable dealing and the rudiments of a code of ethics. The foundation of the whole structure is the specialised technique, and it is the multiplication of these techniques that has made possible the spread of these organisations. To put it briefly, scientific methods have been introduced into non-manual routine work, like that of the secretary, the accountant, the trade statistician, the advertiser, the office manager. These techniques are not, by older standards, professional. They do not call for creative originality, as in the case of the artist and scientist, nor must they be linked with sound human judgement and the power to inspire trust in one's character and personality, as in the case of the lawyer and doctor. They demand accuracy and efficiency along established lines. They are, in fact, the mental equivalent of the manual craftsmanship of the Middle Ages, and they lend themselves in the same way to the establishment of semi-professional associations. But in many respects these groups are indistinguishable from the great body of the salaried employees of trade and industry, the white-collared workers of the middle class. These workers are far removed from the spirit of what Veblen called 'pecuniary and business employments'. They are not an organ, but only an instrument, of capitalism. They have little experience of those motives and incentives which are reputed to make capitalism work, or fail to work, as the case may be. There is no ideological obstacle to their being professionalised, and if they are not professionalised they will, as is frequently said, be proletarianised. The signs in England to-day suggest that we shall see a strengthening and consolidating of the middle class on the basis of a modern type of semi-professionalism.

It is important to notice the effects of these changes on social mobility. An organised profession admits recruits by means of an impartial test of their knowledge and ability. In theory they are selected on merit, but it is merit of a particular kind which usually must be developed and displayed in a particular prescribed way. A narrow road leads into the profession through certain educational institutions. How far this favours social mobility depends on whether those institutions are open to the masses, so that merit can win recognition in all classes. Granted the broadening of the educational ladder typical of modern democracies, the system of the official examination is more favourable to mobility than one of arbitrary appointment or casual promotion. But the chance to move comes early, during school days. Once it has been missed and a career has been started at a non-professional level the whole system of formal qualifications makes movement at a later stage well-nigh impossible.

There is another point. In the church or the army, in law or medicine, a man at the head of his profession is on top of the world. He admits no superiors. But many of these new semi-professions are really subordinate grades placed in the middle of the hierarchy of modern business organisation. The educational ladder leads into them but there is no ladder leading out. The grade above is entered by a different road starting at a different level of the educational system. Social structure, in so far as it reflects occupational structure, is frozen as soon as it emerges from the fluid preparatory stage of schooling. Mobility between generations is increased, but mobility during the working life of one generation is diminished. That appears to be the direction in which things are moving to-day, towards the transfer of individual competitiveness from the economic to the educational world, from the office and workshop to the school and university.

This middle-class group of the lesser professions and the salaried employments has many common features. The interests of its members are technical and administrative rather than financial and speculative. Their fortunes are linked, not to profits, but to employment, and if, as Veblen argued, capitalism is bound to sacrifice the latter to the former, they should be unfriendly towards capitalism. The competitive aspects of the concerns in or for which they work hardly touch them, and competition in their private lives is, as we have just seen, weakened by the spread of professionalism. Their desire is for security in the enjoyment of the status their education has won them. Therefore, although socialism would have no terrors for them once they could get over their fear of the word, communism is anathema, because it means destruction of their middle-class status. If, as seems likely, they shrink from an alliance with the workers, to whom will they turn for leadership? Not, probably, to their capitalist employers and clients. Not, I think, to that competitive professionalism, typified by the medical specialist, the successful barrister, and the fashionable architect, which has such close affinities to the world of finance. The natural place for them to look is in what might be called administrative professionalism, of the type described in our discussion of the social services. It is surprising that Veblen did not pay more attention to this group of occupations. He denounced the destructive activities of business, guided by its interest in 'the vendibility of the

output, not its serviceability for the needs of mankind',
and administering that 'tissue of make-believe' called
credit and finance. He turned for salvation to the realism
of the engineer, 'trained in the stubborn logic of tech-
nology', and believing that 'nothing is real that cannot
be stated in terms of tangible performance'.[1] But the
engineer, though a realist, is not well equipped to judge
of human needs. It cannot be assumed that the welfare
of mankind will be promoted by giving man everything
that machinery makes possible. As Professor J. M. Clark
pointed out when reviewing one of Veblen's books, no
one has ever shown 'how social efficiency can be organised
on a technical basis alone'. Progress 'calls for an evolution
of our scheme of values, not for a "technocracy" which
ignores value'.[2] Veblen should have put the professions
as a whole in the position he assigned to the engineers.
They too are realists, they are relatively free from the
spirit of 'pecuniary and business employments', and in
addition it is their business to study human needs and to
construct a scale of human values. Social efficiency, as
distinct from both business efficiency and mechanical
efficiency, should be, and to an increasing extent is, their
objective. In spite of all their faults, it rests with them,
more than with anyone else, to find for the sick and
suffering democracies a peaceful solution of their problems.

[1] *The Theory of Business Enterprise* (New York, 1904), p. 51, and
The Engineers and the Price System (New York, 1921), p. 75.
[2] Joseph Dorfman, *Thorstein Veblen and His America* (New York,
1934), p. 491.

CPSIA information can be obtained
at www.ICGtesting.com
Printed in the USA
BVHW040007160223
658552BV00005BA/118

9 781014 755599